M000026853

42 Rules to Increase Sales Effectiveness (2nd Edition)

A Practical Guidebook for Sales Reps, Sales Managers and Anyone Looking to Improve their Selling Skills

By Michael Griego

Foreword by Mark Leslie,
Founder/CEO of Veritas Software

E-mail: info@superstarpress.com
20660 Stevens Creek Blvd., Suite 210
Cupertino, CA 95014

Copyright © 2009, 2013 by Michael Griego

All rights reserved. No part of this book shall be reproduced, stored in a retrieval system, or transmitted by any means electronic, mechanical, photocopying, recording, or otherwise without written permission from the publisher.

Published by Super Star Press™, a Happy About® imprint
20660 Stevens Creek Blvd., Suite 210, Cupertino, CA 95014
http://42rules.com

2nd Edition: January 2013
1st Edition: September 2009
Paperback ISBN (2nd Edition): 978-1-60773-107-8 (1-60773-107-X)
Paperback ISBN (1st Edition): 978-1-60773-032-3 (1-60773-032-4)
eBook ISBN: 978-1-60773-033-0 (1-60773-033-2)
Place of Publication: Silicon Valley, California, USA
Library of Congress Number: 2009933797

Trademarks

All terms mentioned in this book that are known to be trademarks or service marks have been appropriately capitalized. Happy About®, nor any of its imprints, can attest to the accuracy of this information. Use of a term in this book should not be regarded as affecting the validity of any trademark or service mark.

Warning and Disclaimer

Every effort has been made to make this book as complete and as accurate as possible. The information provided is on an "as is" basis. The author(s), publisher, and its agents assume no responsibility for errors or omissions nor assume liability or responsibility to any person or entity with respect to any loss or damages arising from the use of information contained herein.

Praise For This Book!

"Mike simplifies the complex process of winning and keeping customers and his anecdotes help personalize the advice. This book is a must read for anyone involved with sales."
John Katsaros, CEO Founder, Internet Research Group

"Mike is a top sales expert and trainer who trained our sales team with great results. I highly recommend this book to anyone who needs to sell."
Michael Yang, Founder & CEO, mySimon.com, Become.com

"Griego's 42 Rules are contemporary, practical and really work. Implementation in our company resulted in improved results and more successful sales professionals. Mike is one of the best salesmen, coaches, consultants and trainer in the business."
Wes Lawrence, Regional President, Key Bank

"Mike is a sales mensch. His book has numerous practical quick tips and tools for sales and management."
Sathvick Krishnamurthy, CEO/President, Voltage Security

"Mike Griego has helped me focus on key areas of selling especially in tough economic environments. As a result of these sales tools, I have fine tuned my sales skills and completed one of my best quarters, earning recognition as the #1 rep out of 300 in the U.S."
Leonard Asuncion, Sr Account Executive, IBM Software Group

"Mike has the ability to translate complex strategies into effective, common sense, sales actions."
Len Ludwig, CEO, Vencore Capital

"Mike's book and rules to increase sales effectiveness are right on the money! Every sales person and sales manager can learn from Mike's experience and improve their sales results in a very short period of time"
Al Powell, VP of Sales, Engate Technology

"Mike Griego fully understands that you never graduate from selling! By following his 42 Rules, you will be educated on the best practices of the sales professional."
Bryan Flanagan, Director, Corp. Training, Zig Ziglar Corporation

"Mike has a straight forward direct approach to sales. This book is a 'must have' for sales and sales management success!"
Karen Turrini, President, Turrini Associates

"It's nice to see Mike put down in words the knowledge he's been sharing as a trainer for so long. Even your best sales person can benefit from this book."
Gregory Chagaris, Co-Founder, Outsell, Inc.

"Mike Griego is a gifted salesperson and sales manager who has encapsulated one of the finest roadmaps I have seen for increasing sales effectiveness. It's a must read for anyone interested in increasing sales!"
Larry Ketchum, National Account Manager, 3M

"We adopted Mike's forecasting methodologies with a client's sales team and it aided us in improving the accuracy of our sales forecast by ten-fold."
Brenda Fox, Founder/CEO, Global Connexus

"This "no nonsense" book reflects Michael Griego's exceptional insight into the art and science of selling; its prescriptive collection of applicable selling principles will increase selling success at any level."
Craig A. Lewis, Partner, One Accord Partners

"This book may be the ultimate blueprint for constructing a successful career in sales—it's that good. Buy it, read it, buy one for a friend. It's both motivational and instructive. It will be a classic."
Nancy Nardin, Founder, SmartSellingTools.com

"Mike's book is straight-forward and concise. Each rule builds on the last to help the salesperson create a plan to "own" their territory and productivity. For management it allows you to double check and "fill-in-the-gaps" relative to tactics and process. Don't create a sales structure without it!"
Chris Bartolo, Director Inside Sales, Contactual

"I've had the good fortune of experiencing the power of these rules first hand under Mike's leadership and coaching. This book now allows me to quickly motivate my own sales team to live and succeed by these rules every day."
Stewart Elliot, VP Sales, Workshare, Inc.

"Mike's sales coaching conveys processes I share with superstars like Lisa Nichols, Bob Proctor, Jack Canfield, Mark Hansen and Tony Robbins. They share them with Fortune 1000 executives. You made the best business read choice of the decade in my opinion."
Berny Dohrmann, Chairman, CEOSpace.net, Radio Show Host

Dedication

To Debbie, my wise, loving and encouraging wife of 30 years, and my wonderful children, Brian, Lisa and Jason, all gifted, strong and highly effective people in their own right. You've all been a blessing and a much loved and appreciated foundation.

Acknowledgments

Thank you to all those people who have led, managed and mentored me in life and business, as well as those whom I have led, managed and mentored over the years. The accumulated experiences add up to allow me enough content to offer back to others.

To some key people who have specifically helped me on this project I am especially grateful. Thank you to Mitchell Levy, who pushed and encouraged the dream and to Laura Lowell, who with grace and competence helped guide the process.

A special thank you to Larry Ketchum and Larry Beckham, my first sales manager role models at The Southwestern Company, and to Skip Miller, a more recent sales manager role model who graciously taught and inspired me.

Thank you to all my customers and clients over the years, for their support, feedback and confidence in me and my company, MXL Partners.

Contents

Contents

Figures

Foreword by Mark Leslie

I got my first sales experience selling shoes in a mall many years ago. I never forgot the fundamentals that went into the various aspects of a fairly simple sales process: engaging suspects and prospects (standing at the front door of the shoe store), qualifying (escorting them to "my" set of seats), questioning (size and style, offering alternatives if out of stock), demonstrating ("Try them on, and walk around. They look good—how do they feel?"), closing ("Do you want to wear them out, or should we wrap them?"). Over the years, in more complex technology environments, I added experiences in hiring and managing salespeople and building organizations that were high-performance selling machines. The fundamentals never changed at the field level, only got more complex. However, the sustaining of sales quality, efficiency and effectiveness across the entire organization became the greater challenge in achieving revenue goals and company success. Indeed, sales effectiveness at the micro and macro level has been the elusive target for many companies in which I have built, managed, advised and invested.

I first met Mike Griego in 2005 in a Palo Alto café. Having retired as CEO and Chairman of the Board at Veritas, I was teaching courses on Entrepreneurship and Sales Organization at Stanford University's Graduate School of Business. Mike, as president/founder of a MXL Partners, a Silicon Valley sales process consulting and training firm, and Stanford MBA alumni himself, had contacted me and requested a meeting to simply meet and compare notes. We had a delightful first meeting and discussed a draft article I was writing on "The Sales Learning

Curve" which was published in the 'Harvard Business Review' in the summer issue of 2006. Mike agreed to review it for me and confirm its conclusions. It was refreshing to discuss the complexities of structuring and managing the modern enterprise sales organization with someone so well versed in all aspects of the world of sales. Mike was as comfortable and experienced in the current trenches of the Silicon Valley field sales environments as he was in the executive management and board rooms of very sophisticated organizations and the sales challenges that faced them.

While the world doesn't necessarily need another sales book, it does need a modern, fresh look at the tools, concepts and principles of sales effectiveness at all levels of an organization in today's marketplace. Mike's new book, '42 Rules to Increase Sales Effectiveness,' is a powerful and quick read for all parties involved in driving sales revenue, from the executive team to the sales and marketing organization. He has well captured the keys to increasing sales effectiveness with a crisp, practical and highly readable book.

I wish this book was available when I started my career. It would no doubt have improved my selling prowess, but also would have developed and guided me as an engineering-oriented executive in validating my intuitive hunches and managing and overseeing the sales side of organizations. I heartily recommend you pull up a chair, grab a cup of coffee, read this book and be ready to re-confirm and even re-think your views of sales and sales effectiveness.

Mark Leslie
Mark Leslie is the Founder of Veritas Software (now Symantec) and served as CEO and Chairman of the Board. During his tenure he grew annual revenues from $95,000 to $1.5 billion. He is currently the managing director of Leslie Ventures, a private investment firm. He is also a lecturer at Stanford's Graduate School of Business where he teaches courses in Entrepreneurship and Sales Organization.

Who Should Read This?

If you are a professional salesperson, sales manager or director, VP of Sales, CEO, any role in Marketing, or anyone supporting selling efforts, this book is for you. If you are a senior executive, consultant, venture capitalist, board member, entrepreneur or aspiring up-and-comer, you should know the updated tools, language and tactics of selling in today's market.

As a professional sales consultant and trainer to Fortune 500 firms and leading Silicon Valley technology firms, I have reduced the keys to sales effectiveness to 42 rules. These rules have been road tested over 28 years of personal sales and management experience and close observation of many salespeople and sales organizations. These rules apply to all selling efforts, from high-tech enterprise sales to non-technology sales.

Why Should You Read This?

Sales isn't rocket science, but it's not ABC simple either. While selling is often either over-engineered or over-simplified, today even the professionals are caught off-guard in a changing world and marketplace. "Old school" is out; new school is in, but with a twist. There are key sales fundamentals that never go out of style but still need a refresh. This book, '42 Rules to Increase Sales Effectiveness,' upgrades and adjusts foundational rules for today's business environment to increase the overall sales effectiveness of individuals or teams.

In '42 Rules to Increase Sales Effectiveness,' you will learn:

- **The Effective Sales Perspective** - 5 rules that will realign your thinking about the role of a salesperson to the customer, product and company.

- **The Effective Sales Process** - 6 rules that will clarify and present the correct way to build a selling process from your customer's buying process, your corresponding sales process and tactical sales playbooks.

- **The Effective Salesperson** - 7 rules that lay out the blueprint for the successful and effective salesperson from their attributes, habits, metrics, formulas, scorecards to even their reading lists.

- **Effective Territory Management** - 6 rules that provide guidance for salespeople and anyone managing salespeople to prioritize and strategically approach and manage territories, channels and forecasts.

- **Effective Sales Communication** - 6 rules applied to various levels of your sales communications, from phone and email actions to practical best practices in structuring elevator pitches, sales messages and talking points.

- **The Effective Sales Meeting** - 6 rules that break down the requirements for your perfect and optimal customer sales call, from power preparation, probing and questioning, to qualification and executive white-boarding.

- **Effective Sales Closing** - 6 rules that get to the heart of effectively bringing your deals to closure, with sales cycle tactics and professional deal management that stands out from discovery to proposal to negotiations.

This book will challenge standard conventions while reinforcing best practices that have gotten lost in the recent advancement of new technologies and modern tools. It's a great read for any professional to confirm that their own "salesmanship" is still on target and appropriately current. Use this as your own handbook to reset on key best-practices for the new day or teach a new generation 42 nuggets and practical applications of this fascinating activity called Sales.

Part I
The Effective Sales Perspective

Sales Effectiveness Begins with Proper Perspective

Whether you run a company, a sales team or a territory, it's time to look in the mirror and make adjustments to how you sell and what you think is good salesmanship.

- Rule 1: Rules Are Meant To Be Broken
- Rule 2: It's Not About You
- Rule 3: It's Not About Your Product
- Rule 4: It's All About Your Customer
- Rule 5: It's Also All About Revenue

1 Rules Are Meant To Be Broken

Use rules with your own applied wisdom and discretion.

Let's be realistic. This book presents rules that really do increase sales effectiveness when applied. These rules are solid and proven over the years in numerous organizations including IBM, Sun Microsystems, Infosys, Gartner Group, Cisco and many other leading technology firms in Silicon Valley. But just as I allow for reasonable flexibility in managing sales organizations (no need to be as ruthless as Alex Baldwin in the movie 'Glengarry Glen Ross') so it is with these rules. Use them with your own applied wisdom and discretion.

I wish I had this book at the beginning of my sales career. In essence I almost did, as I was trained well at The Southwestern Company and IBM Corporation. Nevertheless the conciseness of it all would have been helpful. Likewise, I wish I had this book at the time I first became a sales manager and before my first assignment as a VP of Sales. Many pieces would have fallen together in place sooner without trial and error or without having to cobble together learnings from several mentors, books, and raw experiences. Indeed some of these rules would have made some points in my life simpler and certainly increased sales effectiveness.

Some of these rules will absolutely resonate with you, while others may not. Don't fight that. I honestly believe that the majority will provide you fodder to work with and initiate required readjustment to your own thinking, process, tactics and strategies. In any event, run with what works for you and disregard what does not. After all, in most cases, rules are meant to be broken.

2 It's Not About You

There's nothing like a highly effective and productive salesperson with a heart and sensitivity to others.

We spend much of our life focused on our personal needs, wants and desires. From childhood dreams to target goals in academics, sports and personal relationships, we pretty much spend a large chunk of time thinking about ourselves operating in the world around us. It's natural to carry this self absorption over to our professional lives. Of course, we think, we must focus on ourselves to consciously and effectively "get the job done."

In the Sales world, this pre-occupation with our own concerns can impede our selling efforts. There are potentially three areas where selfish thinking can get in the way of your being at your best. Think about it.

Me vs. my Product - Self-focused thinking plays out in how we consider our product or solution in the marketplace. If I care more about hitting my numbers, enlarging my territory or boosting my personal earnings than about bringing value to customers, I risk coming across as callous and cold to customers and partners and even others inside my company. We've all seen the sales rep who steamrolls the marketing team or support team or speaks of his customers with disdain. There's a fine line between caring for our customers and looking out for ourselves. Learn to see and believe the benefits your product solution brings to customers with you as the conduit. This big picture view brings a healthy perspective to your daily sales effort.

Me vs. my Sales Pitch - Selfish thinking plays out literally in how we approach our prospect or customer on the phone, email or face-to-face. If I really don't consider the person on the other side as a human being with their own wants and needs, I risk a distancing or disconnection in my communications. I may be repeating a script or common sales pitch, but I must recognize that I'm ultimately dealing with a real person with issues, dreams and desires of their own mixed up with a potential need for my products or services (see Rule 4). Approach your pitch with deft caution and a heart.

Me vs. my Customer - Once past the initial approach and now into the sales call or meeting, self-centeredness can also play out in how we personally engage with our customers and prospects throughout the sales call. If I am too self-focused in a customer meeting, I risk spending too much of that meeting on my own concerns; namely, my product offerings rather than my prospect or customer (see Rule 3). As we will find, the customers often cares not a whit about you. The vibe of a self-serving salesperson becomes very clear to a prospect.

When one approaches sales with a healthy and balanced sense of self and care for others, then this rule that "it's not about you" is easy to swallow. Indeed, an effective salesperson carries him or her self with strength, confidence and competence. But there's nothing like a highly effective and productive salesperson with a heart and sensitivity to others. It stands out and customers appreciate it. Even if they can't put their finger on it.

A balanced salesperson (see Rule 12) with an understanding that it's not only about him or herself will have a healthy sense of self relative to their product offerings, selling approach and customer interaction. Combine this perspective with some of the effectiveness tools and rules in this book and you have a winning combination that produces benefits for all parties.

Are you selfish in your sales efforts?

3 It's Not About Your Product

For many reps today, the strong tendency is to speak about their products too much and too soon.

The products sold in the marketplace, whether to businesses or consumers, are broad in scope, complexity and value. As salespeople we are selling commercial and consumer products both domestically and globally, including financial products, real estate, home and personal products, hardware and software solutions, consulting and professional services, to individuals and businesses large and small and ranging from tens to thousands to many millions of dollars in value. In our selling jobs, the products we sell are great, cool, fun, helpful, worthy, comprehensive, leading-edge, powerful and awesome. We spend many hours getting trained on them, learning their features and benefits and being able to articulate use-cases and even demonstrate them ourselves. It's very easy to become focused on the value of our products.

While we've learned in Rule 2 that "It's not about you," I can tell you with assurance that to be effective in sales, it's also not about your products. You might be saying, "But my product really is helpful for businesses and streamlines operations while cutting costs, and it comes in blue." This may all be true, but it's really beside the point. This is one of the toughest lessons for us salespeople to learn.

Certainly we need to know and understand our products and services, as well as articulate the benefits and value they bring to our prospects and customers. But as we will discuss further in Rule 4, our customers have far deeper concerns that are either on the surface clear for all to see, or hidden or even stuffed beneath layers of covering. Of course our products may help and come to the rescue, fixing issues of which our customers were perhaps not fully aware. Again, while not irrelevant, they are only props within a scene in a bigger play. Until we recognize that, we will consistently fall into a trap of focusing our conversations too much on our great products and services, to the detriment of fully providing problem-solving solutions to our customers.

Indeed, for many reps today, the strong tendency is to speak about their products too much and too soon. Jerry, one of the better producing reps on an enterprise sales team, was technically adept and knowledgeable. He prided himself in quickly closing business and moving on to new opportunities. His numbers bore this out. He was one of the top reps in transaction quantity, if not in average deal size. In listening and following Jerry on sales calls, it was clear that Jerry knew his products well and got to them as subject matter quickly in his sales calls and conversations. The customers didn't mind because the product was one that when demonstrated rated a high "wow factor;" that is it quickly impressed and interested customers. Jerry was adept at following up with price quotes and moving the deal to closure. This is all well and good except when one considers the opportunity lost in his hurry to close business and move on. When Jerry was taught to restrain from discussing and demonstrating the product too soon and spend appropriate time (note, not necessarily *too* much time, mind you, in his environment), but time well spent to explore the application of his product to other departmental seats and broader implementation within the IT environment, he increased his average deal size by almost 25%.

Likewise, with those selling less complicated products, while our products are great, our focus still needs to be on the simple use or application of our product. The point is that the product is not the focus, rather it is the application of the product as it addresses the issues, needs and problems of the customer.

Do you speak about your products too much and too soon?

4 It's All About Your Customer

The sun sets and rises with customers whose purchase of products pay the bills.

So if it's not about you the salesperson, and it's not about your products, then what is it all about? Well, who's left? It's all about your customer. In sales, the customer is number 1. The customer rules. The sun rises and sets with customers whose purchase of products pay the bills. This should come as no surprise. Then why do we sometimes forget our focus? Because, of course, it's easy to default to focusing on ourselves and our products.

The best companies get this right. When I worked for IBM early in my career it was ingrained in all of us that the customer came first. IBM is a world-class services, engineering and manufacturing company. It's a world-class sales, service and support organization. Across every plant and field branch office, make no mistake that all efforts evolved around ultimately satisfying customer wants and needs. From my perspective, at IBM, Sales is King, but the Customer is Number 1. All employees moved toward the fulfillment of keeping customers coming in and staying in the fold and growing their relationship with Big Blue.

I've never forgotten how that priority permeated the culture of the organization. While there was a healthy respect for our own products, sales prowess and service reputation, there was an almost reverential feeling toward our existing customers and prospects. This carried over into how we as salespeople approached, serviced and sold to them. It wasn't always perfect, but the culture drove the effort. Even our selling process (in the 1980s) carried the mantle *Customer-Oriented Selling.*

With the correct focus on the customer, the foundation for sales success and thus effectiveness is laid. If we respect our prospects and customers as people rather than as objects of attainment, then we approach, engage, discover, question, negotiate and close them with competent humanity. We do not badger, insult, barrage, belittle, disrespect, manipulate, or take advantage of those whom we, in essence, should seek to serve. I daresay that when we approach our prospects and customers with a servant's heart, a workman's ethic, a quality product at a fair and reasonable price, we become a force to be reckoned with in the marketplace.

I once joined a firm and took over a territory previously managed by a rep who was fired for forging customer signatures on two deals. On my second week on the job I had to go out and apologize to upset customers for these egregious acts by a representative of my company. On top of that, I found out that my firm already had a dubious reputation among some customers in my new territory. Without skipping a beat, I immediately went to work on my own systematic 90-day Customer Rejuvenation Program. I did not "approach and sell" during that period as much as simply "reach out and touch" my prospects and customers with a monthly personal campaign that included letters (this was pre-email), postcards and phone call messages. *Every* prioritized account (see Rule 19) was included in the campaign that was personally managed by me, not by Marketing. I had to control the turnaround effort and put a personal stake in the territory ground as the new sales guy in town. My mailings and messages were upbeat, positive and personal. I held my head high and did not issue blanket apologies for past poor service. I approached prospects and customers with the assumption that whatever concerns they had about the quality of our service and support, those days were past. A new day had come and it started with me and a professional and intelligent introduction to the new team.

By the end of my first full year in the territory I was the #1 sales revenue producer worldwide for the company. My customers loved me because I loved them first.

Do you put your customers first?

5 It's Also All About Revenue

Without sales revenue, it all shuts down.

Taking care of customers goes hand in hand with sales revenue production. And yes, it's also all about revenue. The best way to keep your job as a salesperson or sales manager is to keep hitting the sale numbers. Frankly, the only way that anyone in an organization keeps their job is for the company and salespeople to keep hitting their numbers. Without sales revenue, it all shuts down. A company can lower expenses or raise capital, but if sales revenue is not ultimately forthcoming, then all bets are off, or lost.

I had a sales manager/mentor communicate the following quip to his sales troops whenever they approached him with miscellaneous questions: "Besides revenue, what else is it you wanted to talk about?" He boldly and consistently instilled across the team that it was indeed all about revenue. This may seem so obvious to you, but stop and consider how challenging this rule can be.

There are many moving parts in a sales organization including: sales operations, forecasts, quotas, compensation plans, CRM functionality and utilization, lead generation, sales process, collateral, sales meetings, sales and product training, hiring, firing, territory assignments, customer database, etc. This carries over to the details of the jobs of individual sales contributors and their managers including those mentioned above and other issues relative to customer and internal communications, presentations, demonstrations, proposals, pricing, negotiations, closing, contract administration and collections. Certainly much to keep an individual and team talking and, even with good intentions, easily distracted with important matters besides the ultimate goal, bringing in sales revenue.

It takes a focused effort to do it all well. To care and know about the customer while proficiently knowing your marketplace, products and value proposition is a challenge unto itself. At the same time one must know how to maneuver a deal, whether simple or complex, and appropriately weave in the right resources and support team. The effective sales rep stays focused on all aspects of sales excellence toward the end of closing the customer on an agreement to transact business and purchase a product and service. The world keeps turning and the revenues keep flowing only if the deals keep closing. So stay on it, work it wisely by applying the rules reinforced here. But keep your priorities, because after all, other than hitting your revenue targets, what else is there you wanted to learn about?

Of course it's a fine line for both salespeople and managers alike. It's why you're reading this book. We all want to be better and more effective, and these rules will clarify, remind and teach you the modern fundamentals of sales effectiveness. But the goal of sales *effectiveness* is more sales. Success is hitting numbers. Success is bringing in the revenue. In summary, the correct and effective sales perspective is this: the organization or individual salesperson may be good, intelligent and effective, but if the organization or individual does not bring in the revenue, then something's got to change.

Are you focused on revenue?

Part II
The Effective Sales Process

Clarity of Sales Process Leads to Sales Effectiveness

Every purchase involves a "Buy Cycle" and a "Sales Cycle." Effective selling involves mapping the two and managing the process.

- Rule 6: Target Your Customer
- Rule 7: Know How Your Customer Buys
- Rule 8: Know How Your Customer Makes Decisions
- Rule 9: Develop Your Customer's Buying Milestones
- Rule 10: Develop Your Optimized Sales Process
- Rule 11: Create a Playbook

6 Target Your Customer

Broad targets yield general results; specific targets yield targeted results or even bulls-eyes.

First things first. Before we clarify the selling process, we need to understand our customers. Who are they? Certainly we need to understand the market segment we are addressing, specific audience, industry or vertical, and any further appropriate delineation of our opportunity marketplace. At first blush we say we sell to people in the healthcare industry, we sell to doctors, we sell to the pharmaceutical industry, we sell to people over 30 years old, we sell to manufacturers, to lawyers, to IT departments, to the Fortune 500, to "the Fortune 2000," to anybody or everybody. Of course we have to do better that that.

In effective selling efforts it's absolutely essential to know who we are targeting and why we are targeting certain market segments. Wise companies conduct research and market analysis and segmentation studies to hone in on the sweet spot in the market that will be the focus of their marketing and sales campaigns. Marketing departments evaluate assumptions and market information to determine a product market opportunity in terms of market size, growth, competitive landscape and viable margin. These feed into overall marketing plans for specific products.

Once this foundational work is complete, sales and marketing leadership can start to understand the buying and selling process. Without specific targets, selling is random and not optimized, as the sales process can only be fuzzy and arbitrary.

For instance, a web-based software service providing sales compensation automation is a valued product in the marketplace. Who is the target prospect? Is it the sales VP, is it the CFO, is it the head of the commission accounting team, is it the head of IT applications, or is it someone in HR? Are the target customers start-up companies, those under $50M in revenue, under or over $1B in revenue? Or is it companies that have sales teams under or over 20 reps...50 reps...500 reps? It makes a big difference, doesn't it? Without even somewhat pinpointing the target we end up with a sales team and sales and marketing effort that is scattershot, unfocused and less than fully effective.

Even individual salespeople need to break down the focus of their opportunity set. In Rule 19 we will show a tool for prioritization within our assigned territory and target market. The point here is that broad targets yield general results; specific targets yield targeted results or even bulls-eyes. If I know that I'm to sell to CFOs of companies with revenues of $50M to $1B in the manufacturing marketplace, with at least 50 sales reps, now I can generate the prospect target lists and get to work. My world has now gotten smaller, more focused, and assuming the product is geared toward this "sweet spot," then I'm in a great position to be successful. At least from a target marketing standpoint.

How targeted is your marketplace?

7 Know How Your Customer Buys

Whether they're aware of it or not, all buyers go through a buying process.

Salespeople need to understand how their customers buy. Specifically, how do they actually purchase the products you sell? Our customers are always making decisions about products and services via a tangible buying process. In fact, businesses and consumers go through a defined or non-defined buying process. Whether we're aware of it or not, all buyers go through a natural progression toward an end purchase. If we understand that particular buying process then we can more effectively sell to it.

Several years ago some friends referred me to Palo Alto Metro Sports for new running shoes to fix my pronation problem (caused by my ankles rolling out when I jog). When I walked into the store the salesman approached me and asked me if he could help. I described my problem and he proceeded to clarify and explain to me what pronation was and showed me two columns of shoes on the wall that addressed advanced cushioning and stability. At the same time he asked me questions about how often I run, what kind of surface I ran on, how far I ran, in a sense qualifying me while asking me also the price range I was looking at, certain brands, etc. He then said, "I'll go in the back and find two or three pairs of shoes that fit the type of shoes you're looking for. You can try them on, go outside, run up and down the runway. They'll be in your price band. You can then figure out which pair works best for you and we'll get you out of here in a few minutes. How does that sound to you?" Well, it sounded great. What he was doing was stepping me through a shoe buying process, and essentially taking me through his matching sales cycle. At any point I could have said, "Whoa, I'm really just looking—I'd like to check over at the Stanford Shopping Center." But I said, "Bring me out some shoes and I'll give 'em a try." I purchased a pair and have since purchased my last 10 pairs of running shoes from Palo Alto Metro Sports.

Now that's purchasing at a consumer level. Most of us, whether we're buying refrigerators, other household items, cars, etc., go through a process and, if forced to, can specify the various steps of that process. This process can be documented and applied to any business purchase as well.

In the following chart you can see that there is a **Customer Buying Process** that shows a progression through different stages. Terminology can vary whether it's a consumer or business sale. First there is an initial Interest or Awareness stage followed by an Education or Information Gathering stage where information is gathered, compared and explored. Next is an Evaluation or Demonstration stage where one takes it out for a spin drive or "tries it on for size." Then comes a Justification or Confirmation stage where people conduct some type of financial justification and finally a Decision or Purchase stage where the customer makes a buying decision.

As mentioned, this often goes on without people even knowing consciously that this is happening. Good selling maps a selling process (Rule 10) to an understood buying process. If we know where the customer is going, we can map a process to it and take them along while we manage the sales cycle. Just as the good shoe salesman proactively stepped me through the process, so good salespeople know where their customers are going, how their buyers buy and move them along appropriately. This works for a very simple sale like selling shoes as well as the more sophisticated multi-million dollar complex sales efforts, as we shall soon see. Those who understand this will be way ahead of the curve.

Do you know how your customer buys?

The Customer Buying Process

Figure 1:   The Customer Buying Process

8 Know How Your Customer Makes Decisions

"What's the process for making a decision on this and who would be involved?"

You have learned in Rule 7 that customers go through a **Buying Process**. We are working toward building of a corresponding **Selling Process**, which we will get to in Rule 10. You need to understand how your customer makes buying decisions. What is the process in steps, actions and behavior they go through to make the final buying or purchasing decision?

If a buyer goes through a natural process of initial interest, awareness and then information gathering and education, there is a point to ask a fundamental question that gets at how they are going to make a decision to buy or not. Essentially, in more complex buy/sell situations you would like to ask the following question: "Mr. Prospect, how are you going to make your purchase Go or No-Go decision?" Or put another blunt way: "How and when are you going to make up your mind?"

Now the answer to this question is great information you'd like to have, but there's a better way to ask the question. I call it the **Magic Question**. The Magic Question has a few variations but always contains the **P Word**. That word is *Process*.

The effective way to ask the question is: *Mr. Prospect, what is the process for making a decision on this and who would be involved?* There are two fundamental truths behind this very powerful question. First, every individual or company has a process or steps they go through when making a buy decision (Rule 7). Second, there is always at least one and often more than one individual involved in a purchase decision. You need to know who they are.

This powerful question kills two birds with 15 words. It's quite remarkable. Try it. It's magic. Prospects love to tell you their process for decision-making, but you have use the "P word." Since all companies have processes in place for assessing and purchasing products, equipment and services, they will often melt with this question and open up the proverbial kimono and provide you with very useful information about people, process, decision-makers and power-brokers. As we will discover in Rule 34, identifying the key players involved in the decision-making process is critical. It is often people behind the scenes. The Magic Question effectively draws the information out and sets you up for further movement through the sales cycle.

I was calling on Mary, a manager-level contact of an enterprise organization. Mary agreed to meet with me after a series of phone calls to collect preliminary data and set up a discovery on-premise sales call. When I met her and spoke to her I realized she was junior in status and would be the front screen for other key people in the decision-making process. She was very protective and controlling while implying that she was the Big Cheese on this project. Attempting to gain an insight into the decision-making process, I asked her a question which I knew to be a disaster as soon as it left my lips. I asked, "Mary, are you the decision-maker on this?" I believe the problem was not only in the raw bluntness of the question but also must have been in my tone and body language. It was as if I was implying "Mary, you've got to be kidding me." I could see Mary bristle as she sat up and decisively claimed, "Yes, I am!" I was immediately backed into a corner to deal only with Mary and not able to go around her without further offending her. A much wiser, softer and effective question would have simply been: "Mary, what's the process for making a decision on this type of project and who would be involved?" By the way, I did get the deal that quarter, but it took me another year to get Mary to loosen up with me.

Do you know how your customer makes decisions?

9 Develop Your Customer's Buying Milestones

The careful notation and articulation of the customer's Buying Milestones can separate sales winners from mediocre salespeople.

In Rule 8, you learned the effective use of the Magic Question to uncover not only the decision-making process but also the key players involved in that process. Take careful note of the stated time-frames, milestones and people involved. The careful notation and articulation of the customer's Buying Milestones can separate sales winners from mediocre salespeople.

When the customer answers your question about their process for making a decision and who is involved, they are giving you keys to the kingdom. Their answer can come in very broad and general terms or very specific detail. No matter what they say, you should drill down to the next level of granularity so that you come away with a list of steps, meetings, people, reviews, deadline dates, etc., that not only helps you qualify the situation but gives you tremendous fodder for pertinent and effective follow-up.

For instance, as shown in Rule 7, a **simple customer buying process** moves from 1) Interest to 2) Education to 3) Evaluation to 4) Justification before the 5) Decision stage. In discussions with the customer you will actually find that the customer might describe their decision-making *Process* as follows:

- We're identifying our major needs, requirements and alternatives. (Stage 1)
- We're talking to suppliers or vendors and gathering information. (Stage 2)

- Next we'll set up a test, pilot, evaluation or demonstration. (Stage 3)
- We'll then ask for proposals or quotes from the finalists. (Stage 4)
- Finally we'll make a decision. (Stage 5)

Of course, you're in perfect position to ask for details about time-frames, deadlines, evaluation criteria, etc. based on the logical questions being raised.

In a more **complex customer buying process**, the essential framework is the same but, if you are prudent, you are likely to uncover the following:

- We're identifying/studying major needs, requirements and options. (Stage 1)
- We're gathering information, talking and scoping potential solutions with key vendors, writing and issuing an RFI (Request for Information). (Stage 2)
- We'll then conduct a pilot or POC (Proof of Concept) while making recommendations to the Sponsor on feasibility and required budget, and obtain approval from the Architecture/IT and Budget committees. (Stage 3)
- We'll then write and issue an RFP (Request for Proposal), meet with vendors, evaluate their responses, conduct a formal product Trial with the top two selected vendors. (Stage 4)
- Then we'll make a recommendation to the Evaluation and Executive Committee, perhaps have the Committee meet the selected vendor, re-confirm the budget, CIO approval, Architecture/IT committee, finalize legal terms and conditions and obtain signatures. (Stage 5)

Whether the buying milestones are simple or complex, by capturing them in chronological detail, you are now prepared to look like an outstanding professional salesperson. In understanding the ebb and flow of the customer's decision-making process, you are able to clarify time-frames, identify key individuals you need to meet, understand evaluation processes, budget cycles and approval steps. Your subsequent questions and communications with the customer, as well as with your own internal team, will be crisp, purposeful and aligned with effective sales cycle management. A powerful tool that plays off the collection of the customer's buying milestones is the Customer Decision Plan, further explained in Rule 39 as part of The Effective Close section of this book.

Do you know and fully utilize your customer's buying milestones?

10 Develop Your Optimized Sales Process

Over 90% of firms realize some positive effect from the utilization of a documented sales process.

You've identified your target customer (Rule 6); you know how they purchase products (Rule 7) and you understand specifically their process for making buying decisions (Rules 8 and 9). You now have the basic ingredients for developing an optimized selling process. A selling or sales process is best defined as:

> *Formally defined, proven, customized and repeatable selling steps, processes and systems in which reps are formally trained, expected to use, and consistently monitored for that use, developed either internally or via a commercial offering.*

Market-Partners

Pretty fancy, but true. A key to an effective sales process is the mapping or synching up with a known customer buying process. If we know how our target customer buys and makes decisions, then we can develop a corresponding sales process that mirrors the customer's steps and processes. An example of a sales process and its corresponding buying process as seen in Rule 7 is shown in Figure 2.

While this may seem fairly straightforward, almost 18% of companies are "Random" and have no identified sales process at all.[1] Another 45% are "Informal" and do little more than pay lip service to adherence to a documented sales

---

1. CSO Insights, Sales Performance Optimization Report, 2009.

process. Yes, they teach their reps and have implemented this into their CRM (Customer Relationship Management) system, but they lack the rigor and discipline to back it up. Just under 24% of companies are "Formal" in their approach to implementation of sales process; and 13% are "Dynamic" or what I would categorize as "Optimized." Indeed, without enforcement and reinforcement, sales process cannot achieve the promised benefits. What are those benefits? Over 90% of firms realize some positive effect from the utilization of a documented sales process. In fact, in current research Sales Process Execution was cited as one of the top three reasons for winning business.

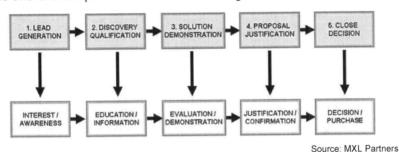

Source: MXL Partners

Figure 2: A Sales Process and Buying Process

Think of it this way: if you're selling a popular product that customers order or purchase without heavy salesperson interaction, then you may get by without the need for a finely honed and documented selling process. But as we've seen, some sales cycles have many moving parts and require a methodical approach to avoid missing key steps and junctures. As salespeople come in various flavors and styles, the key to driving consistent sales effectiveness is the adherence to a well thought out selling process that captures major steps and practices that keep a sales cycle on track.

Sometimes sales success covers up the need for disciplined selling efforts. A fast growing Silicon Valley software company saw revenues increase in spite of an undisciplined and loose sales organization. New management came in and hired consultants to clarify, articulate, educate and ingrain a "new and improved" sales process that guided the worldwide sales organization in best practices that identified key customer personnel and elevated the conversation to a higher level value solution. The result was a more precise sales organization executing improved skills with purpose and rigor. The sales performance did improve with higher value deals and deeper account penetration. Within one year the company was acquired with a very high value multiple.

Have you clarified and optimized your sales process?

11

Create a Playbook

Every selling stage can be dissected into a bullet list of action steps, tactics or strategies.

So now you're ready to document your sales process "playbook." A playbook is just as it sounds—it's a notated game plan of steps, actions and tools used to facilitate the execution of the sales process. In the previous two rules (Rule 9 and Rule 10) we've mapped the selling stages to the buying stages. In Figure 12 (see Appendix A), we've now filled out the specific actions and tools that management has deemed necessary for the salesperson to successfully navigate the sales cycle.

Every selling stage can be dissected into a bullet list of action steps, tactics or strategies. Additionally, specific collateral documents, templates and sales tools come into play at various points along the process.

For instance, at Stage 1—Lead Generation, salespeople are tasked with following up leads inbound from marketing campaigns or websites, or initiating targeted contacts on their own. There is typically some live preliminary lead qualification beyond common lead scoring or form fields. A well-managed sales and marketing team will coordinate specifically what a rep should be doing and document those actions. These are grilled into the sales rep at sales meetings or training sessions. A playbook can be developed for different types of field reps (inside teams, outside direct, etc.) as well as for different product lines (upsell items, renewals, new business sales, etc.).

At Stage 2—Discovery/Qualification, there is ample room for error and inconsistency as reps need to further qualify the opportunity and execute a professional discovery or information gathering sales call. By documenting the specific qualifying and probing questions as well as referencing various helpful sales tools for the rep to utilize, sales management ensures that their team is conducting the right effort at the right time. This continues throughout the rest of the sales cycle.

An enterprise software company's sales team was comprised of inside reps, outside reps and market development/lead generation reps. There were inconsistencies in the quality of customer meetings as reps often generated a proposal (Stage 4) after a single conversation (Stage 1) with the customer/prospect. While sales were closing in some cases, some implementation issues cropped up because the reps had failed to fully scope out the tailored application and use case of the software solution. What was missing was a more detailed discovery/qualification conversation or meeting (Stage 2) and then a planned proof-of-concept (POC) or pilot/trial that solidified the success of the solution but also further developed the customer relationship and growing engagement. The reps were guilty of short-circuiting the appropriate sales process, a common problem in many of today's sales organizations. This problem was alleviated by ingraining through sales training the importance of good sales cycle management and crystallizing the correct actions, tactics and tools.

As noted earlier in the CSO Insights research, approximately two-thirds (63%) of firms fall into the category of Random or Informal when it comes to adhering to a specified sales process methodology.[2] One-third (37%) are Formal or Dynamic when it comes to effectively following some documented sales process.

But today's marketplace landscape requires more than simple documentation and training. "Sales Process 2.0" is all about the dynamic interactivity of sales stages, steps, actions, collateral beyond the printed page. There are some exciting new technology solutions that have taken the concept of "Playbook" to new and powerful levels through the automation of a documented selling process and the just-in-time serving up of the appropriate tool, script, or action-step to guide the new or experienced salesperson. When these tools get implemented across sales organizations around the world, then sales *effectiveness* will meet sales *efficiency* and produce consistent sales *excellence*.

Do you have a Sales Process Playbook?

---

2. CSO Insights, Sales Performance Optimization Report, 2009.

Part III
The Effective Salesperson

Personal Accountability Leads to Personal Sales Effectiveness

"There are two types of people, those who make excuses and those who find a way."
Larry Beckham, The Southwestern Company

- Rule 12: Be a Superstar
- Rule 13: Have a PAR Time
- Rule 14: Make a 10-5-2-Do List
- Rule 15: Measure Activity Metrics
- Rule 16: Develop Your Success Formula
- Rule 17: Keep Score with a Scorecard
- Rule 18: Reading Makes Perfect

12

Be a Superstar

The attributes and make-up of a Sales Superstar are like the balanced five points on a star.

We all like winners and can appreciate superstars when we see them. We admire the superstar athlete who is talented beyond question and helps his team win games. But we've seen superstars come in a variety of packages. Some are boisterous and obnoxious to their teammates, fans and opponents. Others are quiet and gentle, shy and retiring, saving their talking for the gridiron or field of play. Others fall somewhere in between. In all cases there is physical skill, talent, discipline and mental toughness. There are similarities with the superstar salesperson, but with a few variations.

What makes a sales rep a star? Producing results and bringing in the numbers, of course. What do top producing reps, i.e., superstars, all have in common? The attributes and make-up of a **Sales Superstar** are like the balanced five points on a star:

Driver - a self-starter.

The best salespeople are those who need no outside motivation. They possess an inner drive that pushes them to limits beyond the common individual. It's not easily taught. A sales superstar is a natural self-starter.

Technician - technically self-sufficient

The ideal rep can demo the product themselves and only uses technical support for advanced situations or to show team depth. They are knowledgeable about their products and the customer's environment and problems. They are not simply sellers. They are like good customer-facing mechanics that understand how the engine works. They don't necessarily know how to build it, but can talk about its basic function and structure.

Facilitator - manages individual and group communications

A superstar rep is fairly adept in handling discussions one-on-one as well as in one-to-many communications. An excellent rep can command a boardroom full of customer and company representatives and facilitate the discussion appropriately. It's a skill that comes with experience, confidence and sensitivity—clearly possessed by a sales superstar.

Empathizer - can express identification with others

Another key trait of a superstar salesperson is the ability to identify with others and their issues and problems. They genuinely can respond naturally to the stated situation of prospects, customers and their own internal team. This characteristic stems from a sensitive heart and the ability to fully put themselves in the other person's shoes and effectively listen with compassion and empathy.

Servant - a humble and healthy sense of self

Finally, an effective sales superstar is ultimately a server of others, like a servant with a heart, and cares for the other person before themselves. This characteristic really stems from their own security and strong sense of self. They are so comfortable with themselves that they don't have to defend or fight, they actually can care for and desire to serve the other side.

As shown in the diagram below, the attributes and make-up are indeed like the balanced five points on a star. While these gifts and attributes may come naturally to some, they can be honed, developed and fine-tuned. But balance is the key. If any one point is extended or over-exaggerated then the star is off balance. An effective superstar is strong and equally weighted on all superstar points.

Are you a sales superstar?

Figure 3:   The Sales Superstar

13 Have a PAR Time

Effective salesmanship involves discipline and optimized regimens. Most salespeople are challenged in sustaining either.

Salespeople and everyone else in life have the same challenge: getting everything done in a 24-hour day. Effective salesmanship involves discipline and optimized regimens. Most salespeople are challenged in sustaining either. How come successful people seem to accomplish more? Simple. They simply do the things that ineffective, mediocre people do not do or are not willing to do.

On Monday morning when you arrive at your desk what's the first thing you do? You either open up your email and then you check your voice messages, or you check your voice messages and then open up your email. Either way, same result. What happens? You realize that a meeting got rescheduled for 10:00 a.m. that you have to prepare for, or a customer situation blows up and needs your intervention with the service team, or a new sales situation comes up that requires your immediate attention, or etc., etc. By 11:00 am you've had a busy morning working through issues. By 2:00 pm you're tired and look at your To Do list and realize that you've done a bunch of things but have been marching to other people's agenda all day. By 6:00 pm you're exhausted and yet have not gotten a lot of things accomplished that you had intended to get done.

Sound familiar? What happened? How can you stay on track to do the things you need to do?

Institute a **PAR Time** into your routine. PAR Time is a one-hour discipline performed typically first thing in the morning upon arrival at your desk, or it can be done at a coffee shop on your way to work. It is a 3-step personal practice discipline that formalizes and encourages what you already may be doing. Its power however is in the productive use of at least one early hour of your day.

- **PLAN (15 minutes).** Use this time to formalize your day. You plan anyway, mostly haphazardly and inconsistently. Get disciplined about it. Some people over-plan; some do no planning as they just jump into the day. Fifteen minutes is sufficient and substantial to think about and effectively plan out one's day and anticipate all that needs to get done.

- **ACT (30 minutes).** Use this time to tackle a key task or something you've been putting off. Do it, get it started or get it done today. We often have projects before us that will actually take two or four or ten hours to complete. We naturally put these off and will tend toward procrastination if we are not careful. By consciously taking 30 minutes to start or work on an important project or task (proposal, research, letter, territory/account plan, etc.), you actually will find big projects getting done and not stacking up. Big tasks started are easier to complete.

- **READ (15 minutes).** Use this time to catch up on industry publications you've been meaning to read and/or inspirational material on sales and motivation. We all have much to read stacked up on our desktop and computer in-boxes, folders and bookshelves at home and at work. In a sales career, there is much to read (see Rule 18). Salespeople often feel guilty when not on the phone or dealing with customers. It is alright to set aside some time to read; 15 minutes is all we're talking about here. You can accomplish a lot of cumulative reading with just 15 minutes per day.

Incorporate a PAR Time into your daily regime and watch the effect. You will be better prepared, act on the right tasks, and continuously revitalize, grow and develop yourself as a salesperson (and person). All high-achieving people incorporate some type of PAR Time into their daily regimen. Do a reset and maximize your life's routines. One hour a day, that's all we ask!

How are you managing your time?

Make a 10-5-2-Do List

There are four steps to the 10-5-2-Do List.

Everyone keeps To Do lists. No matter the title or occupation, there are daily items to list, remember and get done. In any sales job there are multiple task items that need to be addressed, prioritized and accomplished. If you stop and consider your own experience in optimizing daily personal productivity, the challenge is not in the creation of the To Do list; rather it's the prioritizing and then "Doing" of items on the list. The salesperson or manager that masters his daily To Do's in terms of list generation, prioritization and then effective execution will be the most productive.

Let me introduce you to the **10-5-2-Do List**—the most practical tool you will ever encounter that will make a significant impact on your personal effectiveness, in sales and in life. There are four steps to the **10-5-2-Do List**.

- **Your Top 10** - First write down your *Top 10* "To Do's." You may be saying to yourself, 'I'm a very busy person. I have a lot more than ten items on my list!' That's okay. Go ahead and list out your 20 or so task items, and then immediately stack rank your Top 10. I assure you that when you look at the list there will be a natural prioritization that comes to mind for the top ten tasks to get done today. Make sure you keep your personal task items ("Pick up kids from school" or "Take shirts to laundry," etc.) separate from your work day items ("Make 15 prospecting calls," "Write XYZ proposal," "Prepare for Forecast/Review meeting," "Research the Anderson account," etc.). When you have your Top 10 recognized you're ready for Step 2.

- **Your Priority 5** - Now take a good long stare at your Top 10 list and brutally slash it down to what I call your *Priority 5*. Circle or check off five top priority task items. This is actually very difficult to do. You've already prioritized to a Top 10, now you're reducing that list to a Top 5 which forces you to eliminate some relatively important items off the list. Do not be dismayed; you have every opportunity to come back to these and get them done, we are only whittling down your mountain of tasks to a critical molehill of tasks. When your Priority 5 is itemized, you are ready for the next step.

- **Your Must Do Top 2** - Now stare down the Priority 5 and reduce it down to your *Must Do Top 2*. Think of these final two items as those absolutely critical tasks that have got to be done today or else hammers come down on you. You can't go home today unless these two items get completed. Every one of us has these types of tasks that are up against deadlines, required by management, job-keeping important, etc. Circle or underline your Must Do Top 2. Now you're ready for the final step.

- **Just Do It** - In the words of the great Nike brand slogan, *Just Do It*. Take these two items that you have worked hard to isolate on, and now go get them done. When you have finished these Must Do Top 2 items, then move on to other items on your list in reverse order (Priority 5, then rest of Top 10).

With the **10-5-2-Do List** method, you will find that on some days you will complete everything on your list; on other days you will only get a few items done—but they will at least be your most prioritized and therefore most important task items. The cumulative effect of this daily whittling down of tasks and priorities on your personal productivity is profound. I challenge you to try this for two weeks. I assure you that in those two weeks you will have accomplished more and felt on top of your game more than you have in a long time. 10-5-2-Do. Just do it!

How are you doing with your To Do's?

15 Measure Activity Metrics

Many firms and reps don't know just how valuable these metrics actually are.

When asked how many new prospecting calls the Inside Sales team made each day, the Director of Sales of a client firm proudly stated that every team on her sales team made 40 calls a day. When I asked her how she knew that, she stated confidently that "she hears them" as she sits in the bullpen with them. "They all know that 40 calls is the number of calls they need to make and that's what they do." Oh, really?

This is a common reaction to classic selling activities across organizations. Some manager at some point in the past has declared a number of, you name it, phone calls, demos, meetings, proposals, mailings, etc., etc., that the sales team is to make each hour, day, week, month, or quarter. That becomes the magic number or mantra for the sales organization for a range of time until someone comes along and changes it or challenges it. Many firms and reps don't know just how valuable these metrics actually are, but often they become unrealistic, onerous, or useless hurdles at which the team winks or rolls their eyes.

I learned long ago that every business has key sales **activity metrics**, which once discovered can drive one to consistent excellence in sales performance or management of a team's performance. In every sales territory I've managed I've sought to understand key selling activities, their appropriate dose, and their yield. I recommend setting up a **30-Day Activity Measurement Plan**. There are three steps:

- **Identify 4–6 Top Selling Activities**—actions such as prospecting phone calls, customer meetings, conference calls, demonstrations, emails, proposals, etc. Determine no more than six (you don't want to track too many or you'll defeat the purpose here); no fewer than four. These are actions that you or management have deemed important in the selling process of your product or service.

- **Assign a Relevant Point Value to Each Activity**—for instance, outbound calls might count one point, a meeting might count four points, an outbound email two points, etc. The key is to have a scoring system that is simple and relevant for each of the 4–6 selling activities identified. Don't over-engineer this; keep it simple and on the honor system if tracking a team.

- **Track the Metrics**—now track the metrics daily, weekly and quarterly for each of the selling activities. Look for the patterns, trends and ranges in the metrics. See the diagram below for a sample tracking sheet. After just three weeks of tracking you will see clear patterns and norms. Take these to heart as a realistic snapshot of your real activity.

Remember to keep this exercise simple. Don't over analyze when you're starting out. Get a foundational benchmark and work from there. There's value in the truth. When we conducted an Activity Metric study at that firm doing "40 calls daily" we found that the call volume ranged from 19 to 53 calls per day by the team. The top two reps were making 20 calls daily; the worst performers were making over 40. We captured what the successful reps were doing, replicated it and drove all reps to make at least 25 *high quality* calls per day.

How's your activity tracking?

Activity Metrics

	Pts	J U N E M	T	W	T	F	Total	M	T	W	T	F	Totals
		1	2	3	4	5		8	9	10	11	12	
Phone - Msg Left	1	1	4	7	6	10	28	3	4	7	6	4	24
Phone - Live	3	2	3	3	2	4	14	0	3	3	4	3	13
Meeting - Live	4	1	1	2	0	2	6	3	1	1	2	0	7
Trial/Demos	2	0	2	1	0	1	4	1	2	2	1	2	8
Emails Sent	1	16	10	8	15	10	59	5	6	12	9	15	47
Email Reply	2	1	1	3	2	4	11	1	2	0	0	2	5
Total Daily Points		29	33	40	31	50	183	24	31	36	37	36	164
Ave. Daily Points							36.6					164	32.8
Daily Live Calls		3	4	5	5	6	23	3	4	7	6	6	26
Ave. Daily Calls							4.6					26	5.2

Figure 4: Results of the Activity Metrics Study

Develop Your Success Formula

Drive to always determine key activity metrics leading to a Success Formula.

When I was in college I had a summer job selling books door-to-door with The Southwestern Company of Nashville, Tennessee. In the 1970's this company sold $30M worth of books to families in their homes each summer through 6000 college students recruited from around the country for a summer job that was ridiculously challenging, but rewarding for the daring souls that signed on. The company still operates today around the world with a salesforce made up of college students. One of the great lessons I learned, among many over three summers, was the power of developing Activity Metrics (Rule 15) into a repeatable **Success Formula**.

The Southwestern Company learned through experience and observation that if a student-salesperson knocked on 60 doors in a day, they could get 30 "Mrs. Jones'" to let them "demo" the book. If these 30 demos (no more than 20 minutes at a house) were conducted either at a door, on the porch or in the house, then one or two customers would buy (despite the quality of the salesperson). The metrics of 60 calls, 30 demos, for one or two sales was drilled into our young impressionable heads. If one would work those metrics, then one could pocket $2,500 in cash (after expenses) after a full summer of work. Big money back in the day.

Since this company had been doing this for over 100 years, the Success Formula for a student summer salesperson was as follows:

Success Formula =
60 Doors/Day =
30 Demos/Day =
1 or 2 Sales/Day =
$2500 Earnings

In my first summer after my college sophomore year I followed this formula and earned $2,500 in the summer. I came back and worked another summer with Southwestern after my junior year and received a summer paycheck of $6,500. I came back one more time after graduating from Occidental College and received a paycheck at summer's end for $10,000. The Success Formula worked the same each summer; the only difference was my close rate increased to many more customer sales per day as I improved with experience.

The absolute key to success was the goal to knock on 60 doors each day. Without that achievement then I wouldn't be able to conduct 30 demos which were necessary for closing deals. Many student salespeople fail in that job because they think they can work a half day or knock on 27 doors. If they cut corners, then the metrics fall short and the success formula breaks down. By the way, to get in 60 houses and 30 demos a day, one had to work 13 hour days. Nothing like also learning a good work ethic! We knocked on the first door at 8 a.m. and the last door at 9:30 p.m., 6 days a week. Hard work and strong effort are also keys to any good success formula.

When I got my first territory assignment at IBM in San Francisco, I automatically sought to determine my Success Formula. In my first two years on quota, I made the IBM 100% Club in July and August, whereas most reps achieve their annual quota goals in December or the last day of the year. Throughout my career I continued this drive to always determine key activity metrics leading to a Success Formula. Today I consult companies and teams in determining their formula which might look as follows:

Success Formula =
X Contacts/Period =
Y Meetings/Period =
Z Proposals/Period =
$Q Revenue Target

Do you know your Success Formula?

17

Keep Score with a Scorecard

This can all be
tracked on one
spreadsheet with
monthly or
quarterly
comparisons.

As a salesperson I always wanted to know where I stood relative to my sales peers and compared to my manager's and company's goals and expectations. Just like any player in sports, we have scorecards, stats and records that show us how we stand against competition, ourselves and company targets. When I became a sales manager and VP of Sales, I tracked my team against goals and expectations on issues and areas both "soft" and "hard." This rule is all about keeping score. Let's take a look at a powerful way to keep score with a flexible scorecard. This is not just for sales managers. The enlightened salesperson can apply this to their own personal scorecard.

Years ago I learned from a sales management mentor that achieving a revenue target is a function of two variables, frequency and competency; that is, how often we do some things and how well we do them. Today I call these activities and competencies. In all selling environments there are key designated activities and items of measurement that represent the quality or mastery of performance, or competencies.

Examples of **Activities** to be scored are as follows:

- Number of Prospecting Phone Calls
- Number of New Opportunities entered into CRM
- Number of Face-to-Face Meetings
- Number of Webinars
- Number of Sales Demonstrations

Examples of **Competencies** to be scored are as follows:

* Presentation Skills
* Lead Management
* Sales Messaging
* Territory Management
* Technical Resource Usage
* Product Knowledge

In addition to Sales Performance metrics such as Monthly or Quarterly Bookings and Quarterly or Year-to-Date Quota Attainment, the total number of Activities and Competencies should not be less than 20 items. Not too many, not too few. As it was during my time with IBM, each item should be rated on a scale of 1 to 5 with 1 being "Poor" and 5 being "Excellent." This all can be tracked on one spreadsheet with monthly or quarterly comparisons.

The key to keeping score with a scorecard is to use this management tool as a vehicle for discussion between a salesperson and manager. A sales manager and a salesperson can effectively use a one-page scorecard as a foundation to talk about performance quality, growth, progress, challenge, joy, disappointment and expectations—many of the things a sales manager never gets to speak about with his or her young charges because there is too much focus on quota, numbers and sales revenue.

Are you keeping score with both quantitative and qualitative measurements?

18 Reading Makes Perfect

The cumulative impact of reading 15 minutes daily over the course of a career is profound.

In Rule 13 one of the three components of PAR Time was to spend 15 minutes daily reading industry publications and/or inspirational material on sales and motivation. Indeed the cumulative impact of reading 15 minutes daily over the course of a career is profound. I learned this lesson as a naïve young college student during my first time spent away from home on a summer job.

As explained in Rule 16, I worked for The Southwestern Company of Nashville, Tennessee, as a student salesman. At the beginning of my first summer, after driving into Nashville for one week of sales training with thousands of other students, we were each given a box of materials. Apart from sales scripts and training materials, the box contained three books: 'How to Win Friends and Influence People,' by Dale Carnegie, 'The Magic of Thinking Big,' by Dr. David Swartz, and 'The Greatest Salesman in the World,' by Og Mandino. At that point in my life, I had only vaguely heard of Dale Carnegie and his book; the others were completely foreign to me. We were instructed to spend 15 minutes each morning reading these books between the time we awoke and the time we knocked on the first door at 8 a.m. While my sales roommates thought this suggestion was silly, I wanted to follow the instructions of successful Southwestern managers so I could earn the average $2,500 summer commissions dangled in front of us for successful student salespeople.

I did read those three books that summer. I did earn $2,500, $6,500 and $10,000 in commissions over my three summers' experience. Better yet, I developed the habit of reading good material to get my head and heart right. I've been reading these types of sales, business, motivation and inspirational books 15 minutes every morning since that first summer of 1976. My personal library has expanded greatly over the years. More importantly, my mind has expanded and grown strong and wise through the consistent feeding of good content that educates, stimulates, motivates, encourages and inspires. Indeed, the cumulative effect of consistently reading good material for the profession you have chosen, and your personal life, even only 15 minutes per day, is profound.

In no particular order, here is a list of some of my favorite sales/business books:

- 'The Challenger Sale,' Matt Dixon, Brent Adamson
- 'Strategic Selling,' Robert Miller and Stephen Heiman
- 'The New Strategic Selling,' Stephen Heiman and Donna Sanchez
- 'SPIN Selling,' Neil Rackham
- 'Rethinking the Sales Force,' Neil Rackham
- 'Customer Centric Selling,' Michael T. Bosworth and John R., Holland
- 'Solution Selling,' Michael T. Bosworth
- 'The Secrets of Question Based Selling,' Thomas A. Freese
- 'Crossing the Chasm,' Geoffrey A. Moore
- 'Inside the Tornado,' Geoffrey A. Moore
- 'I.T. Sales Boot Camp,' Brian Giese
- 'The 10 Immutable Laws of Power Selling,' James DeSena
- 'Selling to VITO (the Very Important Top Officer),' Anthony Parinello
- 'How to Get Your Point Across in 30 Seconds or Less,' Milo O. Frank
- 'Selling the Way Your Customer Buys,' M. Sadovsky and J. Caswell
- 'Proactive Sales Management,' William Miller
- 'The Greatest Salesman in the World,' Og Mandino
- 'The Magic of Thinking Big,' David J. Schwartz
- 'First, Break All the Rules,' Marcus Buckingham and Curt Coffman
- 'Crucial Conversations,' K. Patterson, J. Grenny, R. McMillan, A. Switzler
- 'The Five Dysfunctions of a Team,' Patrick Lencioni
- 'Little Red Book of Selling,' Jeffrey Gitomer
- 'Presenting to Win (the Art of Telling Your Story),' Jerry Weissman
- 'Beyond Selling Value,' Mark Shonka and Dan Kosch
- Rain Making (Attracting New Clients), Ford Harding
- 'Selling to Big Companies,' Jill Konrath
- 'Getting to Yes,' Roger Fisher and William Ury
- 'Sales Automation Done Right,' Keith Thompson
- 'Sales and Marketing the Six Sigma Way,' Michael Webb

What's on your reading list?

Part IV
Effective Territory Management

Sales Effectiveness and Territory Management

Effectiveness does not depend solely on how much effort we expend, but on whether or not the effort we expend is on the right thing.

- Rule 19: Prioritize Your Accounts and Opportunities
- Rule 20: Develop a Territory Attack Plan
- Rule 21: Develop a 360° Account Snapshot
- Rule 22: Upgrade Your Account Management
- Rule 23: Manage Your Channels
- Rule 24: Master Your 30-60-90 Day Forecast

Prioritize Your Accounts and Opportunities

The Account Prioritization Matrix concept is deceptively simple.

In my days of selling IBM computer equipment, I sold the first computer to a company called The Nature Company, a retail establishment with several stores in California. As a young sales rep I performed all the right steps in getting the sale closed and set up for implementation with the third-party software provider and the service team. As we often did back then, we celebrated the setup and installation of the system with a bottle of champagne, in this case on a Friday afternoon.

The following Tuesday there was an implementation scheduling meeting with the software company; the next week there was a "kickoff" meeting with the hardware service and support team. For the next five weeks there were meetings at the account dealing with the smooth implementation of the company-wide system. I was at every one of those meetings. As a good sales rep I attended these sessions even though they were not my meetings nor did they require my attendance. In the sixth week I went to lunch with The Nature Company's Director of IT who managed the implementation. He told me he was extremely pleased with the whole experience, that all was going well, that he was pleased with our software recommendation and the service and support team was outstanding, and appreciated my involvement throughout the process. He then said, "But Mike, I have one question for you: Don't you have anything else to do?" He said "It's not like we're going to spend any more money;

it'll take the rest of the year to fully absorb this installation." The question and comment hit me like a ton of bricks. He was absolutely right. I was spending unnecessary time with a comfortable customer when I should have been out finding and selling more new business prospects like The Nature Company. The lesson was not lost on me.

It was the beginning of a process of prioritization of my accounts that has stuck with me as a territory rep, as a sales manager, as a VP of Sales, and as strategic sales consultant and trainer. The Account Prioritization Matrix concept is deceptively simple, using a two dimensional ABC system of classification. This can be set up on a spreadsheet or built into a field variable within your CRM system. First, set up two variables with ABC designations. For instance, one set of variables might be based on the value of current customer revenues, such as A = $100,000+; B = $25,000 to $100,000; and C = $0 to $25,000. The next set of variables might be future potential revenues of a customer over the next 12 months. It could be the same variables, i.e., A = $100,000+; B = $25,000 to $100,000; and C = $0 to $25,000, or variables with differing values. When you align the various combinations you come up with the following:

Rating	Current $$	Future $$
AA	$100K+	$100K+
BA	$25-100K	$100K+
CA	$0-25K	$100K+
AB	$100K+	$25-100K
BB	$25-100K	$25-100K
CB	$0-25K	$25-100K
AC	$100K+	$0-25K
BC	$25-100K	$0-25K
CC	$0-25K	$0-25K

By simply using this particularly variable scale and rating your top 20, 50, 100 accounts, you have begun to prioritize your accounts and opportunities like only a minority of salespeople. For example, the top group with "A" rated "Future" sales revenue over the next 12 months (by your own definition) represents a subset of your account that warrant significant more attention. My account, The Nature Company, would have represented an "AC" rating and would have signaled me to keep them satisfied but not to spend significant time with them over the next 12 months.

Are you effectively prioritizing your accounts and opportunities?

Develop a Territory Attack Plan

There are four basic components.

The worldwide #1 sales rep sat in his office in early January and wondered how he was ever going to repeat his record breaking $1.1M sales result from the previous year. And what do they typically do with #1 sales reps? They shrink their territory and raise their quota! So it was in this case. His 600 assigned accounts got reduced to 400 accounts and his quota went up by 20%. What did he do? He closed the door to his office and spent the next 2½ hours that morning developing a **Territory Attack Plan**. When he emerged he set about executing that plan month-to-month, quarter-to-quarter. By year end he far exceeded his increased quota, hitting sales bookings over $2.4M and was the worldwide #1 sales rep for the second consecutive year. Let me tell you what I did that January morning in my office.

I obtained a summary sales report from accounting and analyzed my previous year's sales transactions. I realized that I had been opportunistic and somewhat random in my working of the territory. With 600 accounts, I essentially reacted and jumped at anything that moved while proactively targeting the biggest names in my customer list. Through sheer hustle and drive I generated enough sales to hit that $1.1M number, whereas at that company no rep had ever sold more than $750K in a year. Even with 400 assigned accounts now, I wanted to blow through that number with a more systematic approach.

I developed a **Territory Attack Plan** that I have since then helped many companies implement. There are four basic components:

Segment the Territory - Whether the territory is assigned by industry, region, product-line or some other classification, break it down into logical segments. I divided my 400 accounts into groupings by industry, revenue size, bookings amount and history, products installed, renewal dates, new business opportunities, etc. This is critical analysis, but keep it simple. Export the data from the CRM and work with it on a spreadsheet.

Prioritize Target Accounts - Then I used the Account Prioritization Matrix (Rule 19) and developed a two-variable matrix like my shown example that prioritized accounts based on past bookings (first variable) and "guestimated" expected bookings (second variable) over the next 12 months. In a spreadsheet one can sort numerous combinations of appropriate variables based on sales cycle time, product type (renewals, new business, custom). The objective is to generate a top priority target list. I conducted this prioritization analysis on only the top 80 of my assigned 400 accounts to keep my focus on the largest opportunities. I later ran separate analyses on the balance of accounts to further prioritize that batch.

Attack the Targets - I then put together an attack plan that included daily, weekly, monthly and quarterly actions and goals. I was careful to spend the appropriate time on the largest opportunities that made sense (AA, BA, CA accounts) per my assumptions. I used past Activity Metrics (Rule 15) to set a daily/weekly calling plan, monthly proposal plans, quarterly travel schedule, industry events coordination, and marketing campaigns for my territory over the course of the year.

Track the Attack - Finally, I set up my own review and reporting of my key Activity Metrics each month and quarter. I tracked my pattern of activity and the yield of those efforts and made monthly and quarterly adjustments. As for any good sports coach, quarter and halftime adjustments are critical. They are based on what transpired against expected goals. When met or underachieved, evaluation and potential adjustment are in order. I tracked my attack like a great coach.

I didn't wait for or expect my manager to do all of this work for me. I relied and directed myself, keeping management informed. It was the self-discipline and self-management that helped develop an introspective sales management view and inspired me to develop and drive my own teams when my management responsibilities expanded.

How's your Territory Attack Plan?

Develop a 360° Account Snapshot

The general who wins a battle makes many calculations before the battle is fought.

In his famous treatise 'The Art of War,' Sun Tzu wrote that "the general who wins a battle makes many calculations before the battle is fought. The general who loses a battle makes but few. By attention to this point, I can foresee who is likely to win or lose." I've always liked this quote because it speaks to the high value of preparation in war and has proven true throughout history. I believe it applies to all things Sales as well. Like war, the sales battlefield requires good planning and tools to prepare for battle.

I've been involved in numerous strategic account reviews that can run for hours and be quite extensive in preparation and follow-up. Over the past 15 years, while I have seen the continued value for these sessions, I see the need for an alternative methodology that may apply for fast moving environments or where "quick and dirty" strategy sessions are appropriate. I've developed an account review process that can be done in 20 minutes on a whiteboard or where the rep and manager can brainstorm up to three accounts in one hour with no preparation. The net result however is a clear and usable game plan for immediate execution and follow-up.

The **360° Account Snapshot** is a simple tool to help us think through all the actions necessary to move an account forward. We can account for issues big and small and then keep them in context with what we are really trying to sell in specific time-frames. It's a practical, useful sales review tool that will help you stay focused on the necessary actions you and others need to immediately take within your major sales accounts.

The **360° Account Snapshot** (see Figure 13 in Appendix A) has three key components: Situation Assessment, Sales Objectives, and Strategies Tactics and Actions. Successful evaluation of these key components results in a clear Solution, identified People, and realistic expectations of Time.

1. Situation Assessment - We start with a quick situational assessment through brainstorming an "Assessment List." Simply list on a whiteboard or paper all of the key issues in bullet form. Then rate each item as a plus (+) or minus (-) as it relates to your efforts. For example:

- New CIO (-)
- Depressed earnings (-)
- IT spending cutbacks (-)
- Completed successful XT5 trial (+)
- Great relationship with SE team (+)

- Competitive equip. installed (-)
- Exec. exposure - Adams Div. (+)
- Dir(s) Attending SIG Conf. (+)
- Plan Q3 storage upgrade (+)
- System Upgrade plan Q4 (+)

2. Sales Objectives - Now be very specific and list what you are trying to sell into this account or group. There may be one product or many products or services. List them out with quantitative sales bookings amounts and time-frames. For example:
- 933X Storage, $45,000 in December 2012
- I Series System Upgrade, $85,000 in April 2013

3. Strategies Tactics and Actions - Now think specifically what appropriate actions you and others need to take and when to take advantage of situations or address obstacles. List these out. This is the basis for your actions over the next week, month, quarter, etc.

- Q4 mtg with CIO and B Johnson
- Set up trial debrief (Sep)
- Deliver comp. piece to Mark (Sep)
- Lunch w/ Karen and SE's (Oct)

- Talk to Bill re SIG Conf. (Oct)
- Meeting w/ Adams Grp IT (Oct)
- Prepare Upgrade Options (Oct)
- New Product Brief w/ Mark (Nov)

The key to a successful 360° Account Snapshot is the effective brainstorming of all potential pros and cons, clarity of sales purpose and time-frame, and specific follow-up activities and actions that can be tracked and reviewed on an ongoing basis.

Can you do a 20-minute account review?

22 Upgrade Your Account Management

Companies are now moving toward dynamic interactive tools that recreate the Strategic Account Plan....

Account review sessions can be formal or informal sessions involving managers, the account rep or team, technical management and any other key individuals participating in the analysis and strategy development of an ongoing account, typically a major account. They may last an hour, a half day or even a full day for very complex situations. At IBM these sessions were often grueling with intense preparation. Nevertheless they were critical to successfully navigating and directing resources in a complex sales situation.

Today many opportunities lend themselves to strategic review, or at least best practice selling efforts. In Rule 21 we reviewed an informal "snapshot" review tool called the 360° Account Snapshot to manually review deals. Companies are now moving toward dynamic interactive tools that recreate the Strategic Account Plan while guiding one along the sales process for all key sales opportunities.

In the 1980's and 1990's there were Miller-Heiman's Strategic Selling Blue Sheets, comprehensive planning documents for managing accounts. There also were Solution Selling documents, Target Account Selling (TAS) planning documents, and a host of other planning sheets that helped guide the process of effective account planning. All of these were variations on a theme including areas for detailing as follows:

• Account Profile

- Opportunity Profile
- People Profile
- Competitive Profile

The one constant with strategic account planning documents is that salespeople hate to fill these out, whether on paper or simply electronic versions baked in the CRM. They complain that these are too long, too detailed, too repetitive with what's in the CRM notes, etc., etc.

Fortunately a new day is here and companies are now moving toward dynamic interactive tools that create the Strategic Account Plan as the account manager moves through an automated "Playbook." These Playbooks extend beyond the CRM opportunity record and now become the interface for all aspects of the sales cycle. As the rep is guided through the process, the Playbook captures the data and produces a summary "deal plan" or strategic account plan. The benefit of these new tools is that they drive optimized behavior while allowing manager and account team to reconvene over the issues and details derived and develop a comprehensive strategic plan without preparation pain and repetitive activities.

There are many new tools that snap onto existing CRM products that provide automation to improve and direct sales best practices for key sales opportunities. Get current and up-to-date with the new technology that upgrades how salespeople manage accounts and organizations maintain consistent sales behavior and quality.

How well do you manage your key opportunities?

23 Manage Your Channels

(It's) about the sold-out commitment to your decisive channels of distribution.

Assuming all things equal, over the years I've seen that the business that's figured out how to get broader distribution captures the most sales, even with an inferior product. You simply give yourself a greater chance to win by putting your product in front of more people. Of course this depends on your marketplace and product. But we can all agree that broader sales distribution coverage yields more "at bats" and therefore increases the odds of sales success. I'm convinced that the challenge is in determining the right channel distribution and the effective equipping for that channel to be successful.

I was with IBM in the 1980's when the midrange systems division began to develop the third-party software network of firms as extensions of its direct salesforce. Over the next several years, IBM developed programs for Value Added Resellers (VARs) and regional partners that augmented local branch office sales. Over time there were adjustments to compensation for the branch salesforce as IBM moved more toward a channel distribution model. Today there is a balanced mix of direct reps (working out of their own home offices) and many reseller partner firms and Independent Software Vendors (ISVs) selling solutions of IBM equipment, software and services.

In CSO Insight's 2009 Sales Performance study of over 1800 firms, sales were divided across various sales channels as follows:

- Direct/Field Sales = 68%
- Indirect/Channel Sales = 12%
- Telesales = 10%
- Internet Sales = 6%
- Other Sales = 4%

Direct Field Sales representatives will never go out of fashion. When asked why their companies continue to rely on a direct sales force, several commented that "they had more visibility into and control over their direct sales reps as compared to channel sales." Getting the right channel mix is optimized over time with constant test and evaluation.

With a commitment to a channel distribution model, here are the **key steps** to effectively setting up a distribution channel network:

- **Channel Design and Profile**—determine and document your channel model and prototype partners by tiers and segments.
- **Target and Recruiting**—qualify, screen and recruit per the profile, measuring success and partner participation versus objectives.
- **Train, Equip and Evaluate**—develop an on-boarding program that engages trains and prepares the recruited and valued partners for success.

These channel partners need to be managed by a channel sales team that is incentivized appropriately in roles that successfully roll out and support the channel program. Channel strategies are crucial and changing with market and competitor movements. Sales leadership needs to stay close to the ground as these movements will drive the mix and effectiveness of your channel strategy.

Are you managing your channels?

24 Master Your 30-60-90 Day Forecast

Remember, it's not just a report, it's a process.

There are two things I ask to look at first when I am brought in as a consultant for a sales organization. The first is the documentation of their sales process (recall from Rule 10 that only 1/3 of firms have this clearly articulated); the second is their sales forecast report, or more specifically, their 30-60-90 day forecast report. These reports tell me everything. I can see how disciplined the sales and marketing teams are; how clear and knowledgeable the management is on their go-to-market strategies, and how tightly managed or not is the pipeline management and forecasting process.

The CEO of a Silicon Valley startup told me that he would potentially need my help if they missed their quarterly number. He showed me a forecast report that had 88 line items of opportunities that his VP of Sales said might happen, though he couldn't say which ones. Only one deal was closed two months into the quarter. I got a call from the CEO in the first week of the next quarter. My first question was, "How many deals did you bring in last quarter?" He said, "Three deals, and one of them wasn't even on the original forecast report!"

I spent the next 60 days working with the CEO, VP, and the Inside Sales and Outside Sales teams in reconstituting their pipeline management and forecasting system. I implemented a **30-60-90 Day Forecast Report** that was extracted out of their CRM system, Salesforce.com. We enforced a mandatory updating of the CRM by Friday noon each week. We reviewed the following report each week by rep at the Monday morning sales meeting, with each rep seeing each other's report. This report has three important components:

- **Sales Process** - reinforced at the top of the report
- **Forecast Items** - those accounts/opportunities that are at Stage 3, 4 or 5
- **Pipeline Items** - those accounts/opportunities that are at Stage 1 or 2.

30-60-90 Day Forecast

Bob Anderson ABC Company Pipeline/Forecast 090109	Sales Cycle:				Sales Process						
	1	Lead Generation	10%	Generate or Follow-up Leads, Initiate Contact, Pre-Qualify, Create Interest via Phone, Email or Brief							
	2	Dicovery Qualification	25%	Probe (Situation, Issues, Consequence, Solution) Qualify (People, Process, Time, Budget, Need)							
	3	Solution Demonstration	50%	Customized Demo, Tailored Presentation, Technical Win, Agreed-to Solution							
Forecast	4	Proposal Justification	75%	Validate and Re-Qualify Opportunity and Solution, Clarify Value/Financial Justification, Present/Deliver							
	5	Close Decision	90%	Closing, Verbal Agreement, Negotiating Terms and Contract Details, Waiting for Signature							

FORECAST

Rep	Account	Contact	Industry	Product	Stage	Jul	Aug	Sep	Oct	Nov	Dec
BA	LGM	Larry Jones		9835	5	$36					
BA	Anderson, Inc.	Jim Backen		9336	4		$85				
BA	Johnson Tools	Bob Smith		Sys. Upg	3			$40			
BA	Hunter Smith	Bill Cook		9336	3			$24			
	TOTALS					$36	$85	$64	$0	$0	$0

PIPELINE

Rep	Account	Contact	Industry	Product	Stage	Jul	Aug	Sep	Oct	Nov	Dec
BA	NPG Tech.	Jim Stevens		Sys. Upg	2			$12			
BA	Taylor, Inc	Tony Taylor		9338	2			$22			
BA	LG & Assoc	M. Anderson		9336	1				$50		
BA	W&S Inc.	Bob Wilson		XP 3000	2					$75	
BA	Beck Enterprises	Louis Tripper		XP 3000	2				$60		
	TOTALS					$0	$0	$34	$110	$75	$0

Figure 5: A 30-60-90 Day Forecast Report

Whereas their previous method was capturing 88 potential deals in play, essentially any deal at any stage, we now enforced a discipline to only "Forecast" deals that had been given a customized demonstration (Stage 3), had received a proposal (Stage 4), or were in closure (Stage 5). In the example shown of Bob's deals, there were now four deals to really bank on, or Forecast; not nine deals.

In the next full quarter, that same sales team "forecasted" 21 deals and closed 18 of them, a company record. The following quarter they forecasted 25 and closed 19, which helped them secure another round of funding.

The 30-60-90 Day Forecast report is not magic, but it does produce results like a good sports coach produces a better team with discipline, rules and accountability. While utilizing terms such as Pipeline, Forecast or Best Case and Commit, this report can be produced out of your CRM. Master the 30-60-90 Day Forecast for yourself or your team. Remember, it's not just a report, it's a process.

How's your forecasting process?

Part V
Effective Sales Communication

The Effective Salesperson is the Great Communicator

Effective sales communicators paint verbal pictures that guide and engage. There is subtle structure, logical flow and purpose to all forms of their communication.

- Rule 25: Elevate Your Sales Pitch
- Rule 26: Develop a 20 to 40 Second Speech
- Rule 27: Live to Sell Another Day
- Rule 28: Manage Your Sales Email
- Rule 29: Get Them to Call Back
- Rule 30: Share a Great Testimonial

Elevate Your Sales Pitch

This is your big chance to make an impression and capture an audience.

In the sales world, one of the most overused terms is the "Elevator Pitch." This actually derives from that proverbial ride on an elevator when someone asks you the question "What do you do?" The idea is to answer the question while you travel only one or two floors on the elevator. In other words, keep it short and sweet, but effective. In the venture capital world, the Elevator Pitch refers to the brief presentation of a business plan or concept.

Actually, we are all often confronted with the need to briefly articulate a message or summary. When we meet new people at the backyard barbeque or other social gatherings we are sure to be asked the question "So, what do you do?" We try to answer in a way that is clear and socially acceptable. In the sales world however, it goes well beyond the "Elevator Pitch." This is not a simple introduction. This is your big chance to make an impression and capture an audience.

To elevate your sales pitch there are three key components that need clear, simple articulation for your business, company or product: **Summary Description**, **Business Credibility**, and **Value Proposition**. If you can nail this down in bulleted, streamlined talking points you will have created the foundation for powerful, consistent and effective sales communication that can be used in a variety of settings as we will find out in other rules in this section.

- **Summary Description** - develop a single sentence or two that summarizes specifically what your company or product does. Example: "XYZ Corp produces software that reconstitutes how companies secure and protect informational content in files, documents, and data stores."

- **Business Credibility** - specify the "bragging points" that give your company or product credibility. Example: "We're the #1 Fastest Growing Security Company" or "We've got four of the top Fortune 10 companies as clients, or "Our technology has eight patents pending."

- **Value Proposition** - articulate what your product does for your target audience in tangible terms. This is another overused and muddled term. Value propositions specify the value that your customers obtain from your product. Example: "Many of our customers experience a 20% reduction in cost savings and a 30% increase in productivity within the first six months of using our solution."

When marketing and sales leadership come together on a succinct description of the business, a clear articulation of key bragging points that show the company and product is legitimate, and targeted value stories that communicate what buyers can expect and experience from your company or product, then the sales pitch is elevated. Careful attention to these components results in effective sales communication.

Has your sales pitch been elevated?

26

Develop a 20 to 40 Second Speech

Credibility can be established in 20 to 40 seconds.

Do you know how long it takes to make a good (or bad) impression? Whether one is on the phone or face-to-face, research shows that it takes between 4 and 6 seconds. Do you know how long it takes to establish credibility? 20 to 40 seconds. The problem with most salespeople is that they don't take full advantage of the 20 to 40 seconds that people will give them. They may make a strong impression in the first few moments but then either talk too long or not long enough. Many a salesperson has picked up the telephone and said something like the following:

> "Hi, this is Bob from Transco Techno-Wizard. We're the premier provider of Techno-Wizards with offices in 27 countries. Our product was voted best in class at the recent Techno conference. Can I show you a demo?"

This is too short (10 seconds) and not overwhelmingly interesting or compelling. This type of approach would invariably lead to a "No thanks, not today" response.

The **20–40 Second Speech** is a simple framework for a highly effective introductory sales pitch. It builds off what was created in Rule 25.

Introduction–Who Am I and What Do We Do?
You've already created a Summary Description. Use this after introducing yourself and your role. This should be crafted to use powerful and effective words that make a clear point.

Credibility–1 to 2 Bragging Points. Again, you've already created bullets of "bragging points" that emphasize your quality and give you credibility. It's okay to brag, only not too long. Only one or two items here. At most three. Don't overdo it. They really don't care; they're only being polite. But use the opportunity to strategically strut your stuff and pass the sniff test.

Problems–One or two Problems Observed. This is the part that is often left out by salespeople. Use this section to voice real problems out there that others like your prospect are having. Of course, problems that your product solves, without talking about your product. For example: "Many executives tell us that consolidating operations and costs while maintaining productivity is a key focus." The key here is to think of common problems your target customers have and which your product solves.

Transition–Open-Ended Question or Call to Action. Now end this little speech and pass the ball over to the prospect to respond to your question or call to action. For example: "I'm wondering if this is something that you are facing too?" Or "I wanted to see if we could meet for coffee and discuss what we've done for others like you."

Here's another way that Bob in our earlier example might have conducted a 20–40 second speech:

(Intro) "Hi, this is Bob from Transco Techno-Wizard, an international tech services firm.

(Credibility) We're the #1 worldwide distributor of Techno-Wizards, the market-leading product recently voted best in class at the recent Techno conference.

(Problems) In speaking to many customers, I'm often asked, "How can I lower my technology costs while improving my overall IT performance? That's a great question.

(Transition) Let me ask you, how are you doing in terms of managing your IT spending in this challenging marketplace?"

This is not a script, but rather a framework for developing talking points to optimize an introductory conversation and take full advantage of the 20 to 40 seconds most prospects will give you. By the way, use your own good judgment on whether it's closer to 20 or 40 seconds. If the prospect on the other end of the phone gruffly answers and growls "Johnson speaking!"—you might want to go with the 20-second version. In any event, you'll sound like a professional and give every prospect a fair chance to understand you, your offering and what it might do for them.

Do you have an effective 20 to 40 second introductory speech?

Live to Sell Another Day

...perhaps the
situation may
change someday
for your
non-interested
prospect.

Whether selling books door-to-door to Mrs. Jones or sophisticated hardware and software solutions to business enterprises, I always was prepared to counter any response from my prospects in early discussions. Sales is not random. Preparation of anticipated situations is key.

Once past the introductory 20–40 Second Speech (Rule 26), the prospect might respond to you in one of three ways. In answering your open-ended transition question the prospect might say:

- "No, I'm not interested" or "This is not a good time" (same thing)
- "That's not really my issue"
- "Okay, tell me more"

In all cases you should be positive and tactful. After all, not everyone buys. There are lots of other fish out there, and perhaps the situation may change someday for your non-interested prospect. As I always say: "Live to sell another day." Let's address how you might respond to each of these scenarios.

Not Interested - The first response of "not interested" requires a counter-response that explores yet doesn't push it. You might respond by simply saying "Okay, sounds like things are in pretty good shape over there. I just wanted to introduce myself to you. We've been quite successful with others like you and thought it might make sense to explore how what we've done for others might possibly work for you and your firm." If they say, "Yes, well thank you for calling anyway." Say a cordial goodbye and say you'll keep them on the list and check back with them later in the year. Most people will not object to that. If they say no to that, then peg them for a call in six months anyway. That person may be gone or you might approach another party. Go to the next prospect. Don't spend your time with non-interested people. Incidentally, if they say that "It's not a good time" it's usually an excuse for lack of interest or understanding. Offer to call back at another time and try to set it up. You will most likely catch their voicemail, at which time you simply give them a powerful 20–40 Second Speech as a voice message.

Maybe - If the response to your open-ended question is "That's not my problem or issue," then the door is open for you to explore and find out just what is the problem. If you're prepared to discuss potentially five or six problems that your target prospects have, again which you know your product addresses, then you can just offer up another problem or two until you find a hit or ask them outright. For example: "Bob, we're dealing with a lot of companies working through a variety of challenges. What are the top two issues that you're facing right now relative to your IT environment?" You'll find this will further draw them out and then you can respond and probe appropriately (See Rule 32 - Become a Probe Master).

Yes - When the customer responds with any answer to your question other than no, then you've got them engaged for next steps. Per your developed sales process playbook (Rule 11) you will then proceed to ask them appropriate questions about their situation and environment, probing and qualifying as you carefully guide the conversation. You might simply set them up for another phone call that will include someone more senior or technical on your end, again per your sales process. Or perhaps invite other people on their end. You are still in the Initiation stage moving toward the Discover stage.

Manage yourself. Be crisp, clear and respectful. Ask natural exploratory questions and respond as your natural inclinations take you. Your confidence will shine through. There will be no pressure or angst on either end of the phone. You have a product to sell; you are simply giving people a fair chance to respond to it and letting the chips fall as they may. Maintain professionalism and live to sell another day!

Are you effectively managing the conversation?

Manage Your Sales Email

What are some of the keys for using email for sales communications?

We've all received the email from a salesperson that was too long or poorly written or both. Perhaps you've written a few like that yourself. With the intent of communicating salient points about a product or service, the writer gets carried away with valid content and information that supposedly will "sell" the product on merits and value. Or what about the use of email to follow up or communicate with prospects or customers throughout the sales cycle? What are some of the keys for using email for sales communications?

I've always believed in the double whammy: the email and phone call, or the phone call and email. I've thought a lot about how I personally respond to salespeople. A salesperson would do well to send an email introducing me to what they are selling and then calling me. They should also leave me a crisp 20–40 Second Speech voice message linking their name to the email I received that day or even a couple days earlier. While there's no guarantee of a sale, their odds go up considerably in getting my attention.

It's even more effective in getting me to remember them if their email incorporates the following **three keys** to email sales communications:

Keep it Short and Simple - Your sales email should ideally be seen on one screen, not so long that one has to scroll several times. This applies to general sales email templates as well as email follow-up and sales correspondence. People do not always read every word. Sentences should be simple, key words should be used, even bolded if appropriate. The 20–40 Second Speech even can be used as a guiding framework to succinctly communicate with a logical flow.

Keep it Personal and Professional - There is a line between our personal and professional lives. A fine line that can be deftly crossed to great effect when communicating with prospects and customers. If in doubt, err on the side of keeping it professional. It's okay with friends and some good comfortable customers, but with a few exceptions most prospects don't really care about your new baby pictures or successful sports exploits of your children. They do appreciate a human touch as long as it is handled appropriately. It's okay to show a human side to your email, but be respectful of your real purposes.

Keep it Reasonable and Relevant - Finally, your email correspondences should relate to the issues at hand. I once received an email on Good Friday from someone selling marketing services. He started out his email by writing that "if I was like (him), then I too probably find Good Friday boring." He went on to say that I should listen in on his webinar featuring a marketing guru with him sharing great marketing strategies. He struck me as a particularly tone deaf marketing expert. While you might say it was relevant as it was sent just prior to Easter weekend, the bold assumption that he wouldn't possibly offend a certain percentage of his audience who took Good Friday seriously was both unreasonable and ignorant.

Email communication can be powerfully effective if the writer is conscientious and wise. For the salesperson, it is critical that one pay extra attention to detail and fundamental keys.

Are you effectively managing your sales emails?

Get Them to Call Back

**It's not
always easy.**

Effective salespeople get people to communicate with them. It's not always easy. You leave a message, send an email, then wait for something, anything that lets you know they know you're there. But they've gone dark on you. It's happened to all of us. It happens even more in tough economic times. What's a salesperson to do?

One thing to do is to be calm and realistic. There are **Three Reasons** why people don't return your calls:

- **You're not compelling.**
  Sorry, but there's a very real chance that your sales pitch or message is just not striking or compelling enough for the prospect to respond. Welcome to the sales club. It's not the end of the world. Change your message if you're finding people are consistently not responding to you.

- **They're too busy.**
  This is most common as people are often interested but are tied up with other projects or issues. Remember that other people have Top 10 lists or even Top 20 lists. You might be #17. They'll get to you eventually. The suggestions below will be most helpful for these busy types.

- **They're not interested.**
  There's a high likelihood that they are just not interested in your product or service. Again, this is not fatal. It happens all the time. Better to have a "No" than a "Maybe" that will waste your time.

Here are some steps to increase the likelihood that prospects or customers return your calls:

Develop a Compelling 20–40 Second Phone Message. Remember in Rule 26 we learned to compose a powerful 20–40 Second Speech. This can be easily adapted to a compelling phone message. There's a logical flow to a crisp message/pitch that hooks one to listen, respect and respond. Note: your email should have the same structure.

Follow up Appropriately. Don't give up too soon, but don't overdo it. Place up to 4 calls over 2 weeks before moving on, or call back next quarter, as appropriate. Keep track of the follow-up details in your CRM. Many salespeople fall short here as they fail to stay systematic in their territory sales activities.

Remember Not Everyone Buys. Some people/companies are just not good prospects right now. Not everyone is ready to buy your products now or potentially ever. But don't blow your chance to even possibly do business with them in the future. Be gracious, professional, and "live to sell another day." (Rule 27)

Are you getting them to call you back?

30

Share a Great Testimonial

**Effective
salespeople have
good stories to
tell and tell them
quite well.**

A great salesperson will have a story to tell for every occasion. Not a story for a story's sake, but a story that can be used as a testimonial at appropriate points throughout the sales cycle. Effective salespeople have good stories to tell and tell them quite well.

Here's an example of a sales testimonial story:

A client had seven call centers providing outsourced services. They wanted to distribute information across the centers via screen pop-ups without requiring software on each desktop. There was a clear lack of IT integration between the various call centers. With (product name) providing real-time event notification, we integrated with their existing browser application and gave them a solution that was half the cost of any alternative and deployed in 90 days. We rolled out the application in four hours at each site without disruption. The CIO told us it was the smoothest implementation he'd ever seen.

There's a **5-point framework** for telling a good sales story. Let's break it down.

1. **Who was the Client?** Due to some confidentiality agreements, you don't have to disclose the name of the client. You can simply reference a customer or client:
   A client…

2. **What was the Situation?** Simply describe the situation and or problem that existed which ultimately gets resolved by your solu-

tion:

...had 7 call centers providing outsourced services. They wanted to distribute information across the centers via screen pop-ups without requiring software on each desktop.

3. **Why was there a Problem?** Specify why the problem existed. This is an opportunity to describe an underlying cause to problems that the prospect might not have thought of before:

   There was a clear lack of IT integration between the various call centers.

4. **How did You Solve It?** Now briefly relate how your product resolved the problem:

   With (product name) providing real-time event notification, we integrated with their existing browser application...

5. **What was the Quantifiable Outcome?** Finally, mention quantifiable results from your solution. Insert a powerful quote if you can as well:

   ...and gave them a solution that was half the cost of any alternative, deployed in 90 days.We rolled out the application in four hours at each site without disruption. The CIO told us it was the smoothest implementation he'd ever seen.

Good testimonial stories come in different sizes. You should have them available at your ready disposal so you can tell a tale of various lengths. The example shown here could be told in 30 seconds or one could go on to tell a longer version up to two minutes long. The effective salesperson is a storyteller. Have your stories ready.

Do you share good testimonial stories?

Part VI
The Effective Sales Meeting

The Keys to Mastering the Customer Sales Call

Effective sales meetings with customers and prospects require preparation and a repeatable game plan that's proven, simple and memorable.

- Rule 31: Prepare the Call Box
- Rule 32: Become a Probe Master
- Rule 33: Qualify, Qualify, Qualify
- Rule 34: Make a Player Chart
- Rule 35: Develop an Executive Whiteboard
- Rule 36: Present Your Solution

Prepare the Call Box

There's power in thinking through the upper and lower acceptable limits of a desired goal.

A sales rep went into the meeting with the IT Director. He had waited three weeks to get this meeting after several calls and messages with his assistant and the Director himself to arrange their schedules. The meeting lasted 45 minutes; the rep thought the call went well. The prospect asked good questions about the product technology and use cases. The rep asked good questions about the prospect's IT environment and experiences, wants and needs in the product area. They parted with an agreement to meet again in another week to see a more detailed demonstration of the product and include some other technical members on both sides. As he walked to his car, the rep's heart sank as he realized he never asked about the CIO or about their budget situation.

Ever leave a sales call and realized that you forgot to collect a very key piece of information or make a particular point which you determined was critical to progressing the sale? We all have. Whether you label it forgetfulness or sloppiness, either way it hinders your selling effort and is completely avoidable.

I recommend a very powerful tool that takes three minutes to prepare and can be done on a piece of paper while waiting in the lobby, sitting in the car, or awaiting a call at your desk. The Call Box tool is all about forcing you to write down key objectives and your expected results. There is something magical about anticipating a range of responses that will invariably better prepare you for your meeting. You will never again forget key questions, points or objectives in a sales meeting. You will be crisper and more professional than most salespeople.

Below is a Call Box. Simply draw a box grid as shown below:

	Best Outcome	Least Acceptable Outcome
Objective 1		
Objective 2		
Objective 3		

Figure 6: A Call Box

Now think of the top three objectives for this meeting you're about to go into. What are the Top 3 things you want to accomplish? You may have more objectives, but use the Call Box to prioritize your Top 3. Here are some examples:

• Get an org chart
• Find out the decision maker
• Find out their real pain
• Set up big meeting with CEO
• Invite them to sponsor event
• Agree to a beta or pilot

Now think of desired outcomes. For each of your three objectives, think through what is the **Best** result and what would be the **Least** (that is, Least Acceptable). For instance, regarding obtaining an organizational chart, the best outcome would be receiving an entire company organizational chart; the least might be just receiving a departmental org chart or even a verbal overview. For finding the decision maker, the best outcome would be getting the name, phone number and email; the least acceptable might be simply getting the name. The point is that you spend a few minutes before the call thinking through the key objectives that you'd like to achieve in the call. There's power in thinking through the upper and lower acceptable limits of a desired goal. Now you've got it in your notes. You can refer to it during the meeting and at the end of the meeting and rest assured you'll never miss an important sales call objective again.

How's your sales call preparation?

32

Become a Probe Master

A fundamental skill in effective selling is the ability to *draw in* the customer while you *draw out* information.

The biggest mistake that sales reps make in sales meetings is mismanaging the discussion flow and failing to appropriately extract enough valuable information from the customer. This is easier said than done. A fundamental skill in effective selling is the ability to *draw in* the customer while you *draw out* information. Mastering the art of the well-executed discovery sales call is really about the asking of effective probing questions that achieve these desired results.

In a customer sales call or meeting, there's a simple and easy to remember framework that will keep you on a logical discussion/questioning path to effective customer discovery. I teach salespeople to interview prospects and customers like a news reporter. Like a good investigative reporter, salespeople need to gather basic foundational information, then further explore the challenge or problem with probing questions. There are four parts to the **Probe Master** framework using the acronym **N.E.W.S.** (see Figure 14 in Appendix A).

1. Now Questions - Information Gathering About Current Situation: First, collect basic background information about their current environment, situation or status. For instance, when I'm meeting a VP or CEO about a possible sales training or sales consulting engagement, my "Now" questions are as follows: *How many sales reps do you have? How many hit their quota last quarter or year? Are they direct or indirect? What* *is their typical profile?* If I'm selling software, my "Now" questions might be: *How many users in the organization? What's your current IT environment?* I need basic data to get "the lay of the land." This is relatively straightforward and easy. Most reps do this fairly well.

2. Explore Questions - Problem Finding: These are open-ended questions meant to uncover key challenges that your customer/prospect is facing. Questions like: *What are your top three departmental challenges? What do you look for in ____? What's the biggest issue relative to ____? What would you like to achieve this quarter?* The key at this point is to resist the very strong temptation to talk about your product. Remember Rule 3! Many reps cannot resist and end up diving into a product discussion before full discovery is done. Hang on tight and move to the next level of questioning.

3. Why Questions - Problem Understanding: In response to the answers to your previous exploratory questions, respond with natural curiosity as to the reasons for the challenges, issues and problems. Understand the Why (and the Who, What, When, Where and How) behind the problem. Questions like: *What do you mean? Why is that? What's going on? What's keeping you from getting there? How are you dealing with that? Are those goals achievable? Who's mostly impacted?* The questions here are about finding the important details and implications of the problems and issues uncovered earlier.
Note: It will be very difficult to resist jumping in and blurting "Our XB1000 Fillibration Oxydizer can reduce that problem by 37% because of our patented hydrogenic biospherous lint de-processor engine." Please do resist. You should simply say, "I believe we might be able to help you. Before getting to that, I'd like to ask you a few more questions." Then go right back into asking more exploratory and understanding questions until you have gathered ample data. Now proceed to the last step.

4. Summary - Reiterate and Confirm Observations. Finally, summarize what you've heard and gain confirmation. You may conclude that you need to meet again and include other parties, or come back with further information, or proceed to the next stage of the process such as a demonstration or product pilot.

Bottom line: if you follow these Probe Master steps you will present yourself as a good and careful listener who asks pertinent questions, who's not pushy with a solution, and who diagnoses before prescribing a fix. These are all very good impressions to leave with a prospect/customer. You will have successfully drawn them in while you've drawn out information. (By the way, these techniques will help in personal relationships too!)

Are you a Probe Master?

33 Qualify, Qualify, Qualify

Early in all sales situations, know the Who, What, When, Where, Why and How.

In addition to good probing skills during the early stages of the sales cycle, qualification skills are fundamental to effective selling. Many a deal has moved down the sales cycle commanding people resources, time and money only to find that the prospect is not fully qualified. I find this a problem in even the most technically savvy and sophisticated Silicon Valley enterprise sales organizations. In our rush to sell and close, we make qualification assumptions only to be surprised later. Like the "Location, Location, Location" mantra in the real estate industry, "Qualify, Qualify, Qualify" is a fundamental principle in effective selling.

In terms of sales prospect qualification, early in all sales situations, know the **Who, What, When, Where, Why and How**. A simple way to track all aspects of effective qualification is to simply track those **Six Qualifying points**. Let's break it down.

1. Who are the People and Competition? You need to understand who are the key contacts that will affect the sale. Rule 34 "Make a Player Chart" will dig into this deeper. Additionally, you need to understand who you're up against competitively. Key questions to ask to uncover this during discovery/probing calls are:

- What's the process for making a decision on this and who would be involved?
- Who are the other companies you are talking to and what's your decision criteria for vendor selection?

2. What is the Opportunity? You the sales person need to be asking yourself just what is the real opportunity here. Is there a defined project? Is there an application fit? Is there a compelling event on which you can capitalize? Additionally, you must think of the application of your various product offerings, and even consider whether the opportunity is too small or beyond your firm's capacity.

3. When is the Date? Every deal has a time-frame for evaluation, decision making, and implementation. Here are some questions to draw this out:

- What is the time-frame?
- What is the target date for a decision?
- What is the implementation date?

4. Where is the Money? Critical to effective qualification of any sales opportunity is the understanding of the existence and source of funds. A few key questions:

- Do you have a budget identified?
- What is the budget process and who would be involved?
- (if they have no budget) What's the process for obtaining funds for a project like this and who would be involved?

5. Why the Buy? Beneath the surface of every deal are the real underlying motivations and reasons driving the decision making. **Consumer** buying decisions focus on Product Features, Quality, Service, Cost and Brand. **Business** buying decisions focus on the Vendor, Product and Services, Price/Cost and ROI, Time, and potentially even the Sales Person. In both consumer or business deals there are typically two of these elements that bubble up as priorities. The way to draw this out is to ask the following question:

- What is your key decision criteria?
- What's most important to you?

6. How Do They Buy? Finally, every company has a process by which they buy. This process includes key people and the power players. By asking the following question you can determine valuable information that will help you throughout the rest of the sales cycle:

- What's the process for making a decision and who would be involved?

Qualifying an opportunity is not done with sequential questions or necessarily in one sales call. Effective qualification is usually done over a series of conversations in the first few stages of the sales process. These six qualification points, easily remembered as Who, What, When Where, Why and How questions, are difference makers in effective selling.

Are you a Qualify Master?

34 Make a Player Chart

A visual mapping of the key contacts in a complex sale can be invaluable.

In every sales transaction there are various people with whom you interact. They include low-level staff, mid-level managers, senior executives, people in finance, procurement or purchasing departments, technical evaluators, end-users and decision makers. If you've ever received professional sales training in your career you know that it's important to know the key buyers, influencers, users and champions in any sales opportunity. Our CRM systems help us keep track of these contacts; however, there's more that can be done to avoid the common mistake of mismanaging the "players" at a prospect/customer account.

The Player Chart works off the very simple concept that key contacts at prospect accounts can be tracked based on their **Position** and **Status** as well as their **Attitudes** and **Perceptions**. Every contact has a title or position in their organization ranging from "junior" to "senior." Likewise they also have certain mindsets about our products and service offerings ranging from "negative" to "positive." On a simple 4-square quadrant these contacts can be placed on an appropriate position on the chart. A visual view of the mapping of the key contacts in a complex sale can be invaluable. Below is a sample of a Player Chart.

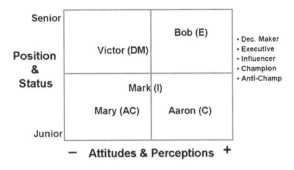

Figure 7: A Sample of a Player Chart

Typically in any complex sale there are various roles that get played such as decision maker, executive, influencer, champion, even anti-champion. You might label these contacts differently or include users and evaluators or economic buyers on some other terms you favor. Simply take the people you're engaged with and place them on the chart per their position/status and their attitudes/perceptions.

This particular chart shows five players. Victor is the Decision Maker (DM) whom we have not met. We don't necessarily know his thoughts about us. Bob is the Executive (E), perhaps our board member knows him personally but we have not leveraged that relationship yet. Mark is an Influencer (I) who at this point is neutral. Mary is a strange one in that she was at the first meeting, but has not been engaged in subsequent meetings and the product demonstration. She is actually an Anti-Champion (AC) and you will eventually find out that she is tight with your competitor and is pushing for a review of their product. Aaron is your Champion (C). He loves you and your product. You spend a lot of time with him as he's helping you maneuver through this organization.

The Player Chart is very revealing. In our example, you can see once it's on paper, we actually have lots of work to do. We really only have Aaron on our side. It's clear that we need to garner more senior support for this project. We should clearly see that there's an opportunity to contact Bob, perhaps to get to Victor if Aaron can't get us there directly. We need to cultivate Mark and re-engage Mary, perhaps conduct a further discovery call with her to understand what's really driving her.

Fortunately, new generation software is building this functionality into playbook tools for managing sales opportunities.But a Player Chart is very powerful and can be simply created with paper and pencil. Keep it simple, honest, and get a clear picture of where you really stand relative to your deal's key players. The Player Chart works.

Can you chart your customer's "players?"

35 Develop an Executive Whiteboard

A sales rep with a well-crafted Executive Whiteboard is a beautiful thing.

The sales rep was in the customer's office for their first meeting. The rep had skillfully probed and qualified the account with questions that gathered quite a bit of data and useful information about the account situation and where problems and issues existed. The rep offered up a provocative statement about the state of the industry relative to new issues of compliance and security management control. Then he motioned to the whiteboard and asked, "May I use your whiteboard?' The customer nodded and then further engaged with the rep over the next 20 minutes as the rep used the whiteboard as a powerful platform to describe the customer's and marketplace challenges with a helpful framework for considering solutions. The meeting ended with the customer considering the rep of significant higher caliber than his predecessor and thinking to himself as he walked him to the door how helpful and enlightening this sales call had actually been.

Very few salespeople utilize the powerful tool of the **Executive Whiteboard**. The concept is simple. First, let's define what it is:

- An executive-level "chalk talk"
- A physical diagram or drawn on a whiteboard
- A logical, visual guide of a conversation
- A vehicle to demonstrate thought-leadership
- A presentation of current state of challenges
- A method to draw out executive response

For example, one company selling anti-virus software to lower level people in IT departments decided to train the sales team to initiate higher level discussions by developing a "whiteboard" conversation. The following is the visual that salespeople were trained to use as a sales call discussion guide.

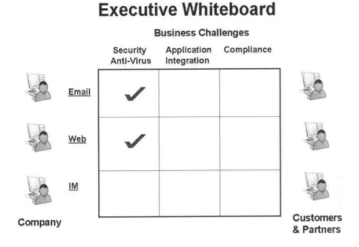

Executive Whiteboard

Business Challenges

Figure 8: A Sample Executive Whiteboard

The objective is to identify and discuss real **business challenges** (Security/Anti-Virus, Application Integration, and Legal Compliance) that current customers are facing. In this example, the focus is communications between companies and their customers and partners. The use of email, the web, and instant messaging (IM) are all channels of communications that present new levels of business challenges. After physically laying the visual on a whiteboard (or piece of paper in front of the customer), the sales rep can simply ask the customer, "So what are the biggest challenges for your organization?"

Getting the customer to engage in "checking off the boxes" with you results in a very strong sales call that reinforces your consultative presence, business knowledge and sales professionalism. You'll notice that there is really no focus on your product offering, only on business challenges. If you can establish your credibility and understanding of the customer's issues first through effective probing and engaging "big picture" discussions of high-level problems, then you are set up to steer the discussion to solutions that address them. A rep with a well-crafted Executive Whiteboard is a beautiful thing.

Can you conduct an Executive Whiteboard discussion?

36 Present Your Solution

On this topic, effectiveness comes from being deliberate, cautious and professional.

As one progresses through the sales cycle, the customers will want to see, touch or try out the product or your recommendation. Effectively managing your product presentation will help you steer clear of common traps and move you and your customer toward the close.

A product demonstration or solution presentation can actually arise in the first three stages of the sales cycle (Rule 10):

Preliminary Demo–Stage 1 or Stage 2. This is common with products that can be downloaded or sent via links or easily discussed and shown while talking to a customer on the phone. This can either be pre-qualification for continuing discussions, or in some cases (simple products) a purchase may result immediately.

Do not confuse this Preliminary Demo with the Stage 3 Full Demonstration. In many software sales situations, a common mistake is to send a quote out after a preliminary demonstration thinking that you've got a hot one that's "ready to close." You're missing out on the opportunity to fully understand the customer's needs. Remember, it's not about your product, it's about the customer (Rules 3 and 4).

Full Demonstration–Stage 3. This is a scheduled meeting (via web conference or face-to-face) often involving technical sales engineers or product support individuals who can demonstrate the product for the prospects and address technical questions. With good prior discovery, this demonstration should be well-tailored for the customer and their application of your solution.

There should really be no surprises for you or the customer during this type of demonstration. If you've done the right discovery and qualification then you've uncovered the issues, challenges, problems and reasons and can align those with your solution. If this meeting is not set up well, then you end up with technical teams on both ends drilling down about technical issues that may derail the sales cycle. Have the right people in the room and objectives clear. If not, this meeting may best be postponed.

"Dog and Pony Show" Presentation–Stage 3 or Stage 4. This is the big one. Many customers will invite the vendor finalists to come in and present a full presentation of their offerings. In this one the full evaluation team should be invited, including key executives and decision makers. This is the opportunity to shine and professionally lay out your tailored solution for their business challenges. Again, this is not about your product; it's about the customer's issues.

Carefully manage the meeting flow. A classic agenda is as follows:
- **Introductions**–all in the room, you and the audience. Some will be meeting you for the first time.
- **Agenda Review**–mutually built and confirmed.
- **Business Problem Review**–what you've learned through discovery and how you plan to address with your solution.
- **Product/Solution Presentation**–live and now customized demonstration or screenshots of application, with relevant stories and tailored comments for customer issues and challenges.
- **Closing Meeting**–immediate strong request for response from attendees, "Robert, what do you like about what you've seen today?" (Note: not what do you think, but what do you like. This will prompt a truer response in a public setting and let you know how you stand.) As you leave, confirm the specific next steps such as "Jim, let's schedule a time next week where I will return and review our written proposal with you."

As shown, the managing of your product presentation is not a simple matter of demonstrating your product. On this topic, effectiveness comes from being deliberate, cautious and professional.

How well are you presenting your solution?

Part VII
The Effective Close

Mastering the Final Stages of Your Sales Process

Effective sales closing is a function of effective sales cycle management and professional and diligent sales practices. There are no short-cuts, only wisdom, hard work and personal integrity.

- Rule 37: Become a Close Master
- Rule 38: Map a Problem Chart
- Rule 39: Use a Customer Decision Plan
- Rule 40: Propose Like a Pro
- Rule 41: Negotiate to Close
- Rule 42: These are My Rules. What are Yours?

37 Become a Close Master

Closing is no more or less than the final culmination of a well-executed sales process.

The closing of the sale is one of the most misunderstood aspects of effective selling. We often picture the quintessential salesman strong-arming a customer with manipulative tactics or sleazy persuasion; or the hyper salesman "going for the close." I once had a manager tell me he simply taught his team the "ABC Method of Sales." I asked him to elaborate and he said that it's all about "Always Be Closing." I felt like saying that he sounded so "1980's." Closing is no more or less than the final culmination of a well-executed sales process. You know when you're there; there should be no surprises or manipulative techniques necessary.

The Close is about resolution and commitment. It is not about tricks, gimmicks and manipulations. Think of it this way: all sales opportunities end up in one of three results. They 1) stall or remain status quo (nothing happens), 2) go to competition, or 3) they close in your favor. What an effective sales rep does is determine as soon as possible which way the deal is going. As the deal moves through the sales cycle there are check points that give one indications that there is still a green light. As each milestone is achieved or hurdle resolved, there is an implicit and explicit commitment to move forward. The effective sales rep is sensitive to these all along the path.

There are **five prerequisites** for a deal to close: Authority, Solution, Urgency, Value and Need. Next to each of these listed below is a corresponding question that directly ties back to what we learned about qualifying in Rule 33.

- **Authority** *(Who* has it and *How* are decisions made?)
- **Solution** *(What* solution is viable and compelling?)
- **Urgency** *(When* is this necessary?)
- **Value** *(Where* is the money to justify the value?)
- **Need** *(Why* is this really being considered?)

If there are any shortcomings in these prerequisites then a deal will not close. If there is any lack of knowledge or understanding to the qualifying questions associated with these prerequisites, then a deal will be inaccurately forecasted. This is why we emphasize with sales teams to *not go past the line* (see diagram below) between Stage 2 and Stage 3 until you have fully qualified the opportunity.

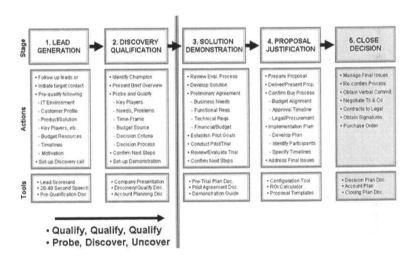

Figure 9: Mastering the Close

Sometimes you will lose to competition, for a variety of reasons beyond your control. But if a deal is stalled or not closing, there is something going on. It is invariably because one or more of the stated prerequisites have been missed. This is always tied to some flaw in the qualification and discovery process. If you want to close more deals, Qualify and conduct Discovery more thoroughly. The following Rules in this final section will augment these Closing fundamentals with tools that support the professional and effective close.

Are you a Close Master?

38 Map a Problem Chart

When done well, the effective sales rep will reveal a tapestry of inter-related issues and causes.

For any department in any industry there are known challenges or problems. For instance, IT departments are constantly seeking seamless applications and reducing costs of operation. Finance departments seek streamline processes that still meet regulatory requirements with fiscal restraint. Marketing seeks well-run programs that meet the needs of the organization and produce tangible results in customer acquisition, revenue effect and customer satisfaction. If you think it through, you can come up with stock problems, challenges and issues that are a given for each target department to which we are selling. Now let's go beyond that and use it for real effective selling and closing.

There are three fundamental truths about our prospects and customers.

- **They have Goals**—these are company-wide, divisional, departmental, and personal.
- **They have Problems**—there are obstacles (problems) that are keeping them from achieving their Goals.
- **There are Reasons**—behind every problem are reasons they exist; some are evident, while others are hidden.

It's the job of the effective salesperson to fully understand the customer's goals, existing business problems and challenges, as well as the reasons and causes of those issues. Once again, the importance of good discovery with effective probing questions (Rule 32) cannot be over-emphasized.

Recall that "Now" and "Exploratory" questions about the current environment, situation and challenges will begin to outline the goals and problems in an organization. "Why" questions probe into the reasons why and how these issues impact the organization. When done well, the effective sales rep will reveal a tapestry of inter-related issues and causes. This is all the better for applying your solution as a potential fix.

In this probing and discovery process you can begin to map out a **Problem Chart** as shown in the sample below.

Problem Chart

	Problem	Reason 1	Reason 2	Reason 3
CEO	EPS Decreasing	Eroding Profits	Missing Revenues	Low Customer Satisfaction
CFO	Eroding Profits	Missing Revenues	Old Technology	Unmet User Needs
VP Sales	Missing Revenue	Low Customer Satisfaction	Old Technology	Manual Processes
CIO	Unmet User Needs	Old Technology	Manual Processes	Staff Cuts
VP Mrkt	Low Customer Satisfaction	Staff Cuts	Declining Programs	Unmet User Needs

Figure 10:   A Sample of a Problem Chart

You can start a Problem Chart with standard broad-level problems and reasons that we know from experience in various industries. You can then tailor this to reflect the specific Key Players (Rule 34) with whom you are engaging. The important connection to make is the inter-relationships that these problems have across the various departments. They also will reveal the differing perspectives on the problems you are uncovering. You, as effective salesperson, will be seen to be wise and knowledgeable about various facets of the organizations. As you work through the final stages of the sale you will be armed with valuable fodder for your executive presentation, proposal write-up and closing negotiations.

Can you develop a customer Problem Chart?

Use a Customer Decision Plan

This now becomes a mutually important working document throughout the sales cycle.

There were five vendors competing for the business of a billion dollar organization. The solutions were similar but one vendor stuck out like a sore thumb and won the business. The sales rep was able to differentiate herself from the others in a subtle yet powerfully effective way —she developed and used a **Customer Decision Plan.**

As discussed in Rule 33, one of the most effective questions in qualifying an opportunity and finding out the key players and decision-making process is as follows: "What's the process for making a decision on this and who would be involved?" Another key qualifying question is in uncovering information about the budget: "What's the budget process and who would be involved?" Both of these questions utilize the magic word "**Process**." Again, every customer has a Process by which they do things. The amazing thing about this word is that when you use it in a powerful question as stated the customers melt and start telling you everything you'd want to know about their internal processes. It's like they're so happy to tell someone about that which they know so well and work within. Try it; again you'll be struck by the uncanny power of the "P" word.

In your early Stage Two discussions, while you're conducting discovery and qualification, take good notes on the decision-making and budgetary processes they describe. This becomes the content for your Customer Decision Plan.

The **Customer Decision Plan** is a statement of the sequence of events or activities throughout the sales cycle, as articulated by the customer and discussed with the rep. These are work items or tasks that need to get done, meetings that need to happen, introductions to be made, milestones and dates that are known or need to be established, and finally decision-making dates and the implementation time-table. The following is an example of a Decision Plan:

Customer Decision Plan

ACTION	PARTICIPANTS	SCHEDULED DATE	COMPLETION DATE
Conduct Proof of Concept	VP, Sales Ops, IT	10/16/12	
Evaluate Results	VP, Sales Ops	11/13/12	
Finalists Presentations	VP, Sales Ops	11/30/12	
Final Vendor Selection	VP - Sales Ops, Sales Rep	12/7/12	
Procurement / Legal Review	Legal, Sales Rep	12/14/12	
Complete Reference Calls	Sales Ops	12/14/12	
Executive Meeting - Budget Approval	VP - Sales Ops, CEO, COO, CFO	12/18/12	
Begin Implementation	TBD	1/15/13	

Figure 11:   An Example of a Decision Plan

These plans can be informally stated in an email, a document or a spreadsheet. It is to be sent to your key contact and hopefully Champion/Executive for input and approval. This now becomes a mutually important working document throughout the sales cycle.

The sales rep selling to that billion-dollar organization used this method in articulating back to the key contact all that had been discussed relative to the decision-making and budgeting processes. From the very first meeting, this rep stood out amongst her competitive peers in her professionalism, thoroughness, and listening skills. The key customer contact said that she held him accountable for each milestone and in essence helped him "keep the project on track and do his job well." With a Decision Plan as a consistent guide, she effectively closed a significant contract with this significant customer.

Are you utilizing a Customer Decision Plan?

Propose Like a Pro

You will never go wrong if you capture best practices and then institutionalize them.

So when does the proposal really come into play? You may have given out pricing information, or at least a price range early in your discussions. Now what is the appropriate way to propose your solution? When do you use the standard 12-page boilerplate document versus something less formal? How do you avoid the common mistake salespeople make when it comes to sending out proposals?

Most companies have a corporate proposal template. I find that most of these templates are non-current and verbose. There is a time for the boilerplate document, or at least some pages from it, but the effective rep carefully streamlines this proposal template to be something that he or she can stand behind and accurately reflects the professionalism they themselves project.

As a rule, I always go to the top producing reps and ask them for their two versions of proposals and at least two versions of their email cover notes. Every good rep has at least two versions, a short and long version that they have cobbled together over time. By asking up to three reps for their versions, I can capture the best practices and begin to see how they are presenting to the outside world. I will always find one that has it nailed; that is, they have captured and honed the optimized short and long versions. If I'm a new rep, then copy their tactics. If I'm a VP or consultant, I then work to institutionalize these versions and find out from marketing or sales leadership where we went astray. You will never go wrong if you capture best practices and then institutionalize them.

There are **four key points** to understand in proposing to customers:

1. **Preliminary Proposals are Good** - In many cases it is absolutely appropriate to give a preliminary quote to a prospect while still early in the sales cycle (Stage 1 or 2). Give a broad range. I've answered the proverbial question "How much will this cost?" with the following: "Well, it depends—we have customers spending a few thousand to up over six figures. Do you have a budget identified?" Their response will dictate whether they are in the ball park of an opportunity to pursue.

2. **People Like Options** - In both preliminary verbal quotes or particularly in informal written quote ranges, people respond well to options. Good-Better-Best; Small-Medium-Large; A-B-C.; Low-Medium-High. You can easily present a range of prices that essentially keep you in the game while hopefully drawing out the prospect's budget leanings and attraction toward either the low or high end.

3. **Deliver in Person or Review on the Phone** - One way to lose control of the sales cycle is to hand over a proposal by sending it in an email or direct mail. Ever send one out and then have the customer go quiet on you and disappear? Best practice is to set up a customer office meeting or phone call in which you explain and review your proposal section by section. Many a deal has gone awry because a proposal has not been fully read or understood.

4. **Don't Deliver Your Proposal Before it's Time** - A common misstep is to deliver a proposal too soon after only a brief conversation or two. Be conscious of your sales process. You may think you have enough to go on to deliver a quote. Maybe. But in a more complex sale you must go through your sales process paces to fully discover and uncover all you will need to understand and prepare a comprehensive proposal of substance. I've seen too many reps send out quotes before due diligence is complete and end up with a stalled deal, or a lost deal because their competitor managed the process more professionally.

Be a professional in all aspects of the sale. Proposals do matter. With attention to detail you too can propose like a pro.

Do you propose like a professional?

Negotiate to Close

Sales negotiations need not be contentious or Machiavellian.

A final aspect to effective closing is negotiation. This is another area that is often misconstrued as both salespeople and customers believe they must dig in their heels to protect themselves from being "out-negotiated." Sales negotiations need not be contentious or Machiavellian. One must be on top of their game and be conscious that all negotiations are toward closure. However, the effective salesperson thinks of the other side and behaves with dignity and respect for themselves and their customer. There is no dishonesty or win-lose mentality. There is only a win for both sides after carefully considering both sides of the equation.

Good sales negotiations move through a natural **4-Step Process**. By clearly understanding and anticipating these steps and when to deploy them, the effective rep wisely negotiates all through the sales process. These steps also apply to a specific scheduled negotiation session, for instance, with purchasing or legal departments.

1. **Understanding Issues and Objectives** - This is really an offshoot of all the good discovery that is done in the early sales stages. By careful listening and note-taking and use of Problem and Decision-Making tools, the rep should be armed with a clear understanding of all the issues on the table for both sides. Knowing that often both sides do not view issues the same way, it is best to

compile a pertinent list of key variables. Sample variables are: price/budget, qualify, time-frame, support, packing, utilization, product features and project application.

2. **Analysis and Clarification** - Again, prior sales meetings draw out key answers to well-asked questions. In a negotiation meeting, there is the give and take of questioning and the seeking of clarification. There may be a break for both sides to evaluate and assess their positions. At this point it is helpful for analysis to be able to stack-rank the issue variables from your perspective as well as how you believe the other side would rank them.

3. **Resistance and Compromise** - It is to be expected that some resistance will arise and therefore a need for compromise. Anticipate the range of tolerance for both parties. For instance, think through your "walk-away" point and consider what theirs would be. Also, consider your "best deal" scenario as well as their "best deal" scenario. By doing so you will realize how difficult these negotiations may be and what it might take to reach a compromise.

4. **Settlement and Confirmation** - When the deal is finalized, do not gloat or mope. The deal is done. If you've done the right job in preparation and understanding of the issues and variables on both sides, you should be able to put together a deal that makes sense for all. As in non-business relationships and dealings, it is considerably better to lose a little bit on the negotiation table and keep the relationship, than to lose the relationship and win the lion's share of the deal.

Again, as we stated way back in Rule 2, It's Not About You. Clearly in sales negotiations you do want the best deal possible, but not at the expense of your reputation or the goodwill and favor of your customer. The most successful negotiations are those that make both sides feel like winners. Again, take the high road and live to sell another day. You will sleep better, you'll gain the respect of your customers and peers, and you'll know you've done the right thing in the treatment of others. In my book you will have increased your sales effectiveness.

Are you effective in your sales negotiations?

42

These are My Rules. What are Yours?

You've got the template.

There is less than five minutes left in the 4th quarter of a high school championship football game. The score is tied 7-7. The All-American tailback catches the punt at the 50-yard line and returns the ball to the 5-yard line. On first-and-goal the quarterback in the huddle calls for a "Pop Right"—a play in which he takes the snap from center, turns to the right and hands the ball off to the team's All League fullback who dives into the gap between the right guard and right tackle. The play is stopped cold for no gain. On second-down the quarterback calls the same play. This time the fullback runs to the three-yard line.

It's now third-and-goal. With the clock running, the quarterback calls for a "Pop Left"—the same identical play except to the left side of the line. As they approach the line of scrimmage, the left guard glances at the left tackle and they both nod their heads, as if to signal "it's now our turn." As the left guard gets into his 3-point stance he recalls all the blocking fundamentals that have been ingrained into his head by his coaches for many hours over years of practice. Stay low, explode into your man, drive the legs, dig, dig, dig, don't stop until the whistle blows....

When I think about it, I can still smell the grass as I lay face down in it, my chest across the goal line, that All-League fullback lying over my shoulder holding the ball. I was the left guard. We scored the touchdown. We won the game. We won the championship.

Like all those football blocking fundamentals, this book has included tools, concepts and fundamentals for effective selling and sales management. It's really on you, the reader, to pull this all together as appropriate and apply it to the big tasks in front of you. In many cases, much is at stake, even more than high school championship games. The clear memory I have was the flashing across my mind, at the exact moment of truth, all that I had learned and practiced to make me effective at that needed time. May it be so for you as well with all that is in this book. May you step up to the occasion and implement all tools and fundamentals necessary for you to be at your best, to sell and execute effectively and successfully in your own high stakes game. I'll be cheering for you.

This book has broken down the key areas of sales effectiveness. From the Effective Sales Perspective, Process, Salesperson, Territory Management, Communication, Sales Meeting, and Close, these rules apply for both salespeople and managers alike. You should re-read these rules and recalibrate them appropriately for your own environment.

You've got the template. Now rewrite or make your own rules. Let's start a discussion. Join me and my blog at www.42rules.com/michaelgriego.

A Diagrams

Sales Process "Playbook"

Stage	1. LEAD GENERATION	2. DISCOVERY QUALIFICATION	3. SOLUTION DEMONSTRATION	4. PROPOSAL JUSTIFICATION	5. CLOSE DECISION
Actions	• Follow-up leads • Initiate contact • Pre-qualify • Set-up Discovery	• Identify Champion • Present Overview • Probe and Qualify • Confirm Next Steps • Set-up Demonstration	• Evaluation Process • Develop Solution • Prelim. Agreement • Pilot Goals • Conduct Pilot/Trial • Evaluate Trial • Confirm Next Steps	• Prepare Proposal • Del/Present Prop. • Confirm Process • Implementation • Address Issues	• Final Issues • Confirm Process • Verbal Commit. • Negotiate Ts & Cs • Contracts to Legal • Obtain Signatures • Purchase Order
Tools	• 20-40 Second Pitch • Pre-Qualify Doc	• Discovery Doc • Account Plan Doc	• Pre-Trial Plan Doc. • Demonstration Guide	• ROI Calculator • Proposal Template	• Decision Plan Doc. • Closing Plan Doc.
Stage	INTEREST / AWARENESS	EDUCATION / INFORMATION	EVALUATION / DEMONSTRATION	JUSTIFICATION / CONFIRMATION	DECISION / PURCHASE

The Customer Buying Process

Source: MXL Partners

Figure 12:   A Documented Sales Process

360° Account Snapshot

Figure 13: *A 360° Account Snapshot*

Probe Master (NEWS)

Diagnose Before you Prescribe

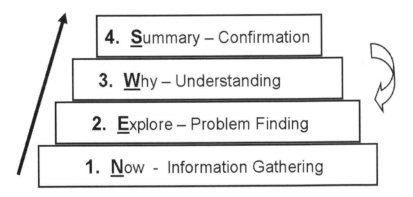

Source: MXL Partners

Figure 14: *The Probe Master*

About the Author

Michael Griego is president of **MXL Partners**, a sales consulting firm providing organizational sales training and strategic sales management and coaching services.

Michael conducts executive, sales and sales management consulting and training services for companies around the world. He brings over 28 years of practical high-technology sales and sales management experience to his clients. He has held sales and executive management positions with IBM Corporation, XL-Datacomp/StorageTek, Dataquest/Gartner Group, Zona Research/ Intelliquest, Active Decisions and Workshare.

Michael has conducted sales training and consulting services for a wide range of companies from Fortune 500 firms to early-stage start-ups in Silicon Valley. He's a popular corporate and CEO summit keynote speaker and guest lecturer at leading business schools including Stanford's Graduate School of Business. Michael has a BA from Occidental College and an MBA from Stanford University. He has been married to his wife, Debbie, for 33 years. They have three children and reside in Mountain View, California.

42 Rules Program

A lot of people would like to write a book, but only a few actually do. Finding a publisher, and distributing and marketing the book are challenges that prevent even the most ambitious authors from getting started.

If you want to be a successful author, we'll provide you the tools to help make it happen. Start today by completing a book proposal at our website http://42rules.com/write/.

For more information, email info@superstarpress.com or call 408-257-3000.

Other Happy About Books

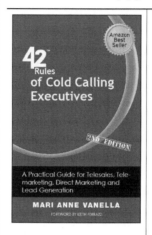

42 Rules™ of Cold Calling Executives

42 Rules of Cold Calling Executives' is an easy to read book that gives concise, easy to implement methods to get results with cold calls.

Paperback: $19.95
eBook: $14.45

42 Rules™ for Growing Enterprise Revenue

This collection of practical ideas about the strategies that raise sales combines Lilian Shirman's observations from almost 20 years of experience in marketing, business development, strategic alliance management and operations with stories and lessons from other technology business leaders.

Paperback: $19.95
eBook: $14.95

42 Rules of Marketing

Compilation of ideas, theories, and practical approaches to marketing challenges that marketers know they should do, but don't always have the time or patience to do

Paperback: $19.95
eBook: $14.95

Happy About an Extra Hour Every Day

The book includes about 300 practical time management tips and everybody should be able to find at least 50 tips that work in one's every day life.

Paperback: $19.95
eBook: $14.95

Purchase these books at Happy About
http://happyabout.com/
or at other online and physical bookstores.

A Message From Super Star Press™

Thank you for your purchase of this 42 Rules Series book. It is available online at: http://happyabout.com/42rules/increasesaleseffectiveness.php or at other online and physical bookstores. To learn more about contributing to books in the 42 Rules series, check out http://superstarpress.com.

Please contact us for quantity discounts at sales@superstarpress.com.

If you want to be informed by email of upcoming books, please email bookupdate@superstarpress.com.

More Praise for 42 Rules to Increase Sales Effectiveness

"Mike Griego provides a practical guide for the sales professional. His 42 Rules offer a methodology that take the mystery out of sales success and will most certainly increase sales effectiveness."
Richard Schultz, VP WW Sales, Sensage

"Mike Griego has the gift of turning the complex world of sales into a remarkably simple and results oriented approach. This is a must read!"
Brian Golter, CEO, Brian Golter & Associates

"Mike has a down-to-earth business approach that really delivers results. Simply put, his rules work and his book puts it all together in one place. This is an important book for any one looking to increase sales and profitability."
David White, President, SC Palo Alto

"This is a must read for CEO's and sales professionals. I've worked with Mike —his strategic insights and practical approach return great value."
Barbara Angius, Managing Director, Accelent Consulting

"42 gems that any entrepreneur can use to build the company of their dreams. Customer-centered, old-fashioned proven strategies meet new school with a twist. Easy to read and filled with inspiring examples that break down the secrets of Mike's unbelievable sales success."
Natasha Deganello Giraudie, CEO Founder, Songline

"This book is most definitely a valuable read! It is chocked full of insightful nuggets of information that every salesperson will find beneficial."
Amie Chilson, Real Estate Broker

"The perfect guide for all salespeople who are hungry for repeatable success! An excellent well written guide that de-mystifies the process for repeatable sales success!"
Chris Holmes, VP Business Development

"Mike has written the essential book for modern sales professionals. His book provides practical, actionable and effective techniques guaranteed to increase the performance of your sales team. This book is not an academic exercise but the hard won lessons of a true sales professional. A must read for those interested in achieving sales excellence in these challenging times."
David Green, CEO, Creative-Spark, Inc.

"We are now using Mike and his successful sales approach. It is great to now add this Best Practice Guide to our Sales Tool Kits."
John Ruggles, SVP Global Sales, Frost & Sullivan

"Mike shares a lifetime of successful sales, sales management and sales training experience and encapsulates it into one extremely practical guide to effective sales."
Craig Olson, VP Marketing